Our Beliefs

I0542780

Questions and Answers by
Āyatullāh Mīrza
Jawād Tabrīzī

AL-BURĀQ

Copyright

Copyright © 2023 al-Burāq Publications.
All rights reserved. No part of this publication may be reproduced, distributed, or transmitted in any form or by any means, including photocopying, recording, or other electronic or mechanical methods, without the prior written permission of the publisher, except in the case of brief quotations embodied in critical reviews and certain other noncommercial uses permitted by copyright law. For permission requests, write to the publisher, addressed "Attention: Permissions [Our Beliefs: Questions and Answers by Āyatullāh Mīrza Jawād Tabrīzī]," at the email address below.

ISBN: 978-1-956276-40-4
Printed and published by al-Burāq Publications.
Translated and annotated by al-Burāq Publications.

Ordering Information
We offer discounts and promotions for wholesale purchases, non-profit organizations, and other educational institutions. Contact us at the email below for further information.

www.al-Buraq.org
publications@al-Buraq.org

First Edition | June 2023

Dedication

The publication of this book was made possible through the generous support of our donors.

Please recite *Sūrat al-Fātihah* and ask God for the Divine reward (*thawāb*) to be conferred upon the donors and also the souls of all the deceased in whose memory their loved ones have contributed graciously towards the publication of *Our Beliefs: Questions and Answers by Āyatullāh Mīrza Jawād Tabrīzī.*

We begin by giving all praise and thanks to God ﷻ for giving us the *tawfīq* to translate this book. He has guided us and without Him, we would not have been guided to the straight path embodied by the Prophet Muḥammad ﷺ and the Ahl al-Bayt عليهم السلام.

This book is dedicated to all the scholars, martyrs and believers who worked tirelessly to promote the pure Muḥammadan path.

We want to also give our thanks and appreciation to all believers from around the world and acknowledge the team which helped al-Burāq Publications complete this work, spending countless hours to make its publication possible. Please recite Sūrat al-Fātiḥah on behalf of them, their families, and their marḥūmīn.

This book is dedicated in honor of the following individuals. Please remember them in your prayers and may God ﷻ have mercy on them and their loved ones.

Abbas

Achoo Dada

Afsheen Z. Kazmi

Alam Ara

Ali Ftouni

Ali Hussain

Ali Khoyee

Alya Agemy

Amina Begum

Bande Khuda

Basheerunnisa Begum

Farrukh Jafri

Farrukh Jehan Begum

Fāṭimah Kaneez

Fidahussein K Rajani

Hajj Haidar Alaouie

Hajj Ahmad Sheet

Hajj Ahmad Taleb

Hajj Hassan Sobh

Hajj Mustafa Kdouh

Hajj Sami Ftouni

Hajj Sobhi Bezzi

Hajji Amneh Sobh-Ftouni

Mortada Ghanem

Musharaf Fāṭimah

Nafees Khan

Naji M. Fenwick

Nisaar Fāṭimah

Qasimhasan

Razia Sarfaraz

Rutênio Araújo

Sabiha Nurul H. Jafri

Sakeena Schultz

Salam Tahir

Sami Saleh

Sardar

Sayed Shehlum

Sayyid Khaled A. Saleh

Sayyid Sobh H. Sobh

Shabeeh ul Hassan Rizvi

Shahīd Ibrahim Hadi

Shujaa Abbas

Siddiqa Jafri

Somo Saad Ali

Syed Fidvi Ali

Syed Iqbal Rizvi

Hajji Hiam Hojeije
Hajji Khadijah F. Taleb
Hajji Khaireh Nasser
Hajji Zahra Kunyar
Humayun Ali Baig
Hussain Shaheedi
Huzoor Nawab Rizvi
Ismael Bazzi
Ivan Garcia
Kaneez Kizilbash
Kokab Moradi
Leila Mansour
Majeeda Moosavi
Maleka Begum
Mehmoona Khatoon
Mir Afzal A. Razvi
Mirza Ahmed A. Baig
Mirza Mazher A. Baig
Mohamed P. Walji
Mohammad A. Jafri
Mohsin Abbas
Syed Mujtaba Ahmed
Syed Mujtaba Rizvi
Syed Nawab Zaidi
Syed Nurul H. Jafri
Syed Tilmiz Rizvi
Syed Yousuf Hussain
Syeda Batool
Syeda Maqsooda Khatoon
Syeda Masooma Begum
Syeda Mrs. Iqbal
Syeda Surata Sultana
Syeda Waheeda Moosavi
Taqia Naqvi
Turfah Sobh
Umm Askia
Yaseen Kizilbash
Zahia Srour
Zainab
Zainab Khatoon
Zaynab Todd

Du'ā' al-Ḥujjah

اللهم كن لوليك الحجة بن الحسن صلواتك
عليه وعلى آبائه في هذه الساعة وفي كل
ساعة وليا وحافظا وقائدا وناصرا ودليلا
وعينا حتى تسكنه أرضك طوعا وتمتعه فيها طويلا

O God, be, for Your representative, the Ḥujjat (proof), son of al-Ḥasan, Your blessings be upon him and his forefathers, in this hour and in every hour: a guardian, a protector, a leader, a helper, a proof, and an eye - until You make him live on the Earth, in obedience (to You), and cause him to live in it for a long time.

Terms of Respect

The following Arabic phrases have been used throughout this book in their respective places to show the reverence which the noble personalities deserve.

عزّ وجلّ

Used for God, meaning:
Exalted and Sublime (Perfect) is He

صلى الله عليه وآله

Used for Prophet Muḥammad, meaning:
Blessings from God be upon him and his family

عليه السلام

Used for a man (singular) of a high status, meaning:
Peace be upon him

عليها السلام

Used for a woman (singular) of a high status, meaning:
Peace be upon her

عليهما السلام

Used for men/women (dual) of a high status, meaning:
Peace be upon them both

عليهم السلام

Used for men and/or women (plural) of a high status, meaning:
Peace be upon them all

عجّل الله تعالى فرجه الشريف

Used for Imām Muḥammad al-Mahdī, meaning:
May God hasten his return

قدّس سرّه

Used for a deceased scholar, meaning:
May his resting [burial] place remain pure

Transliteration Table

The method of transliteration of Islamic terminology from the Arabic language has been carried out according to the standard transliteration table below.

ء	ʾ	ر	r	ف	f
ا	a	ز	z	ق	q
ب	b	س	s	ك	k
ت	t	ش	sh	ل	l
ث	th	ص	ṣ	م	m
ج	j	ض	ḍ	ن	n
ح	ḥ	ط	ṭ	و	w
خ	kh	ظ	ẓ	ه	h
د	d	ع	ʿ	ي	y
ذ	dh	غ	gh		
Long Vowels					
ا	ā	و	ū	ي	ī
Short Vowels					
ـَ	a	ـُ	u	ـِ	i

Table of Contents

About the Author

Āyatullāh Mīrzā Jawād Tabrīzī ⚚ (b. 1926-7 - d. 2006) was a Shīʿī authority (*marjaʿ*) and an influential teacher of the Seminary of Qom. During his education in Qom and Najaf, he attended the lectures of scholars such as Āyatullāh Sayyid Ḥusayn Burūjirdī ⚚, Āyatullāh Ḥujjat ⚚, Sayyid ʿAbd al-Hādī Shīrāzī ⚚, and Āyatullāh Sayyid Abū al-Qāsim Mūsawī Khūʾī ⚚. He later joined the Istiftāʾāt Office (office of answering fatwas) of Āyatullāh Khūʾī ⚚ in ʿIrāq.

After Saddam's order to deport Irānians from ʿIrāq, Āyatullāh Mīrzā Jawād Tabrīzī ⚚ had to leave and return to Irān after 23 years of stay in ʿIrāq. He continued his scholarships in Qom. After the death of Āyatullāh Arākī ⚚, he was announced by Jāmiʿat Mudarrisīn as one of the seven Shīʿī authorities.

Āyatullāh Mīrzā Jawād Tabrīzī ⚚ wrote many books in Shīʿī fiqh (jurisprudence), the most important of which is his *Irshād al-Ṭālib* (a four-volume commentary on Shaykh Murtaḍā b. Muḥammad al-Ansārī's ⚚ *al-Makāsib al-Muḥarramah*).

Birth and Family

Āyatullāh Mīrzā Jawād Tabrīzī ﷺ was born in ~1926-1927 in Tabrīz. His father, Hajj 'Alī Kūbar, was a well-known Azerbaijan businessman known for his faith and fairness. His mother, Mirzā Khānum Fāṭimah Sulṭān, was from a well-known Sayyid family in the city.

Education

In Tabrīz

He entered modern schools at the age of 7. He studied until the second year of high school and then went to an Islamic seminary school. He said:

"Some of our friends in high school who wanted to improve their Arabic spent a few hours a day at the Islamic seminary of Ṭālbiyah in the bazār of Tabrīz. They studied Arabic morphology (*ṣarf*) and grammar (*naḥw*) with the teacher of Arabic literature. I accompanied them for a few days and attended the lectures on Arabic literature. However, what happened to me was not so much the improvement of my Arabic as the passion for the Islamic seminary. It opened my fate, and I chose to become a scholar (eventually becoming a *marji'*)."

When he made such a decision, he encountered opposition from his family, since in that period, the Islamic seminary and the clergy were under pressure and underwent many troubles. Upon his insistence, his father was convinced, and thus, he chose to become a scholar, though he had the opportunity to be a successful businessman. He left home and spent all his time in the seminary school of Ṭālbiyah. He studied Arabic literature, eloquence (*ma'ānī*), rhetoric (*bayān*), and parts of jurisprudence (*fiqh*), and principles of jurisprudence (*uṣūl al-fiqh*).

During this period, he was friends with 'Allamah Ja'farī ﷺ. About this part of his life, he said:

"Since I went to the seminary school despite my family's objections, I did not want them to be aware of my problems and thus affect my will to continue my studies. Sometimes my economic problems were so dire that the late Muḥammad Taqī Ja'farī and I had no food for two days."

In Qom

In 1327 AH/1948-9, Āyatullāh Tabrīzī ﷷ moved to Qom, where he stayed for seven years. In this period, the Islamic Seminary of Qom had just flourished. Āyatullāh Burujirdi ﷷ had made Qom the center of Islamic seminaries, and the lectures there were remarkably thriving. Tabrīzī stayed in Faydiyya School and started teaching while attending the lectures of prominent figures. Āyatullāh Burujirdi ﷷ respected him. He said:

"I was teaching *al-Lum'a* and *Qawānīn al-uṣūl* in a masjid in Astana Square. I was an examiner on behalf of Āyatullāh Burūjirdī ﷷ."

Āyatullāh Tabrīzī ﷷ attended the lectures of Āyatullāh Ḥujjat ﷷ in Qom for four years and was spiritually and morally influenced by him. In that period, Āyatullāh Ḥujjat ﷷ was well-known for his asceticism and moral character. At the same time, Āyatullāh Tabrīzī ﷷ attended the lectures of Āyatullāh Burūjirdī ﷷ for seven years. He moved to Najaf despite the teaching opportunities he had in Qom.

In al-ʿAtabāt al-Muqaddasah

It was a great dream for Āyatullāh Tabrīzī قدس سره to go to al-ʿAtabāt al-Muqaddasah and the Islamic Seminary of Najaf. He had the dream ever since he was in the Islamic seminary of Tabrīz, but the dream seemed unachievable to him because of certain problems. One day he attended a scholarly meeting where a religious businessman had relationships with scholars. The businessman offered his support for Āyatullāh Tabrīzī قدس سره, and thus, he provided the means of his immigration to Najaf. He said:

"I was sitting in the Fayḍīyya School and was thinking about the immigration to Najaf. A familiar man I had seen before came to me at that time. He asked: "What are you thinking about?" and I said: "about moving to al-ʿAtabāt". "What prevents you from going there?" he asked. "The circumstances", I replied, "have changed". Muḥammad Muṣaddīq had just fallen in that period, and the Irānian government was so strict with the clergy. "Do not worry", he said. He received some documents and photos from me, and after only a few days, he got me a passport. As soon as I received the passport, I did not wait. I went to 'Irāq with the first possible means. I needed more time to inform my students about my decision."

Āyatullāh Tabrīzī a قدس سره rrived in Najaf when he was 27 years old. With the help of Mīrzā 'Alī Gharawī قدس سره, who had lived in Najaf for years, he resided in the School of Qawām al-Salṭānah Shīrāzī. He began his lively, vivacious days in the Islamic Seminary of Najaf. Since he had entered the Islamic Seminary School at an older age than usual, he doubled his efforts and attended numerous lectures. He said:

"I did not have any vacations for 40 years. I ignored everything and avoided many pleasures to achieve my goals."

Teachers

Āyatullāh Tabrīzī قدس سره attended the lectures of prominent scholars, such as Sayyid 'Abd al-Hādī Shīrāzī قدس سره and Āyatullāh Sayyid Abū al-Qāsim Mūsawī Khū'ī قدس سره. He attracted the attention of his teachers in his early years. He was honored by Āyatullāh Khū'ī قدس سره when he saw his talent and efforts. Thus, he turned into a close student of Āyatullāh Khū'ī قدس سره.

Āyatullāh Khū'ī قدس سره later appointed Āyatullāh Tabrīzī قدس سره as a member of his fatwa office. He was in the office, attended Āyatullāh Khū'ī's lectures, and taught intermediate and advanced courses in Najaf for about 20 years.

He also attended the lectures of Āyatullāh Sayyid Muḥsin al-Ṭabātabā'ī al-Ḥakīm قدس سره and Abū al-Ḥasan Mishkīnī قدس سره.

In addition to obtaining the degree of *Ijtihād* in *fiqh* and *Uṣūl al-Fiqh*, Āyatullāh Tabrīzī قدس سره worked hard on philosophy, the exegesis of the Qur'an, and rijal and mastered these disciplines. His classmates include Āyatullāh Shahīd Sayyid Muḥammad Bāqir al-Ṣadr قدس سره, Shaykh Mujtabā Lankarānī قدس سره, Shaykh Ṣadra al-Dīn Bādkūbī قدس سره, Āyatullāh Ḥusayn Waḥīd Khurāsānī, Āyatullāh Sayyid 'Alī Ḥusaynī Sīstānī, and Shaykh 'Alī Aṣghar Shāhrūdī قدس سره.

Return to Iran

In 1976-1977, the 'Irāqī government increased its pressures against Irānians. The government identified and deported people like Āyatullāh Tabrīzī قدس سره, a prominent figure. Thus, after 23 years, he and several other Irānians had to leave 'Irāq. His compulsory return to Iran saddened Āyatullāh Khū'ī ⚰.

Teaching at the Islamic Seminary of Qom

The fiqh course of Āyatullāh Tabrīzī ⚰ in Masjid Aʿẓam, Qom.

When he returned to Irān and settled in Qom, he started to teach *Rijāl*, *Uṣūl al-Fiqh* (Shīʿī legal theory), and *Fiqh* (jurisprudence). Because of his long-term companionship with prominent teachers in Najaf, his courses were similar to courses in Najaf.

As a Shīʿī Authority

When Āyatullāh Khū'ī ⚰ passed away, several scholars asked Āyatullāh Tabrīzī ⚰ to undertake the Shīʿī authority (*marjiʿiyyah*). However, he was reluctant to do so. Jāmiʿat Mudarrisīn's announcement of seven people, including him, as Shīʿī authorities, as well as his followers outside Irān, such as Sūrīyah (Syria), Lubnān (Lebanon), Kuwayt (Kuwait), Baḥrayn (Bahrain), 'Irāq, as well as some European countries, Australia, and Africa, forced him to undertake the responsibility.

Social Services

The social services of Āyatullāh Tabrīzī قدس سره include the construction of mosques, helping people in need, and building a clinic in Qom. The clinic is medically exceptionally equipped. Āyatullāh Tabrīzī قدس سره commissioned some people to identify the poor and the orphans and provide food and clothes for them.

Demise

After an illness, Āyatullāh Tabrīzī قدس سره died on Monday, November 20, 2006 (Shawwāl 28, 1427 AH). On Wednesday, November 22, 2006, he was buried in the Holy Shrine of Lady Fāṭimah Maʿsūmah عليها السلام after a funeral and Ṣalāt al-Janāzah (funeral prayer) by Āyatullāh Ḥusayn Waḥīd Khurāsānī. Other Shīʿī authorities and figures from Kuwayt, Baḥrayn, Qaṭar, Imārāt (Emirates), Lubnān, Sūrīyah, and Saʿūdīyah (Saudi Arabia) attended his funeral.

After Āyatullāh Tabrīzī's ﷲ death, the Supreme Leader of the Islamic Republic of Iran, Āyatullāh Khāmina'ī, issued a message of condolences in which he characterized Āyatullāh Tabrīzī as one of the most prominent teachers of the Islamic Seminary of Qom whose piety and down-to-earth comportments made him popular among the youths.

Preamble

بسم الله الرحمن الرحيم

In the Name of God, the Beneficent, the Merciful

In light of the spread of spiteful Wahhabism and its dissemination of corrupt theologies in different forms and onto expansive territories across the world, and since it has adopted the strategy of instilling doubt and skepticism about other beliefs, which led to the rise of several inquiries and doubts within the minds of some Muslim youth – especially those who live in Western countries, and due to the need of addressing these inquiries properly and firmly, we decided to compile and raise them before jurists. After a while, we received responses from the religious Marjiʿ (religious authority), Āyatullāh Mīrza Jawād Tabrīzī, who is one of the most prominent Taqlīd references and teachers of advanced religious studies at the seminary. We then found it appropriate to share these responses so that the general public could benefit from them; they are accurate responses based on scientific premises and strong foundations.

We ask God ﷻ to grant us success in our pursuit.

Questions & Answers

Intercession

Question 1:

Some authors say that when God ﷻ says:

﴿وَلا يَشفَعونَ إِلّا لِمَنِ ارتَضىٰ﴾

﴾*wa-lā yashfaʿūna ʾillā li-mani rtaḍā*﴿

﴾*and they do not intercede except for someone He approves of*﴿[1]

He means that if someone is God-pleasing and deserving of His forgiveness, then God ﷻ honors His Prophet ﷺ by accepting his intercession for this person. Meanwhile, he is not granted this intercession if he does not please God. Intercession is a virtual position; what some Gnostics say regarding the fact that we cannot speak to God ﷻ leads us to seek nearness to God through the Imāms – as intermediaries – is false. The truth is that there is not any veil that separates us from God ﷻ.

What is your opinion about this saying? Is it aligned with the Shīʿī theological belief?

---

[1] Sūrat al-Anbiyāʾ, Verse 28.

Answer:

In the name of God, the Exalted.

The intended meaning behind that noble verse is its exoteric one, that is, asking the right-owner to overlook the shortcoming of the transgressor and refrain from punishing him as a form of honoring the intercessor and his position. For, overlooking this shortcoming is good according to sensible and rational individuals, in which case intercession is not a virtual matter.

Whereby the exterior of the noble verse implies those above, it is considered evidence that a rational or narrative proof can only refute. The intellect does not find any barrier against the inclusivity of God's ﷻ mercy to sinners using the Prophet and Imāms' ﷺ intercession as a form of honoring them due to their esteemed position in the eyes of God ﷻ and their life-long dedication to spreading religion, propagating its provisions and making its words superior. Accepting intercession – or any form of pardon – is considered a bounty bestowed upon a person and not a right he has earned.

Moreover, the intended meaning behind the verse is the approval of his religion. For, a divine pardon does not include a polytheist; as God ﷻ says:

﴿إِنَّ اللَّهَ لا يَغْفِرُ أَنْ يُشْرَكَ بِهِ﴾

﴿ʾinna llāha lā yaghfiru ʾan yushraka bihī﴾

﴿Indeed God does not forgive that any partner should be ascribed to Him﴾[2]

And as mentioned above, the intended meaning behind 'approval' does not indicate the entitlement of this person to enter Heaven.

As for narrative proofs, the narrations mentioned on behalf of the Prophet ﷺ and the Imāms عليهم السلام are plenty – nay, they are *Mutawātir* (frequently mentioned) and therefore indisputable. This is the Shīʿī theology which is based on verses and noble ḥadīths; by which any violation thereof would result in deviating from the Shīʿī theology.

---

[2] Sūrat al-Nisāʾ, Verse 48.

Creational Guardianship

Question 2:

Some authors say: The entirety of the Noble Qur'ān is proof of the absence of a creational guardianship (*al-Wilāyat al-Takwīnīyat*) since it says:

﴿قُل لا أَملِكُ لِنَفسي نَفعًا وَلا ضَرًّا إِلّا ما شاءَ اللَّهُ﴾

﴾*qul lā 'amliku li-nafsī naf'an wa-lā ḍarran 'illā mā shā'a llāhu*﴿

﴾Say, *'I have no control over any benefit for myself nor [over] any harm except what God may wish*﴿[3]

Had the prophets acquired a creational guardianship, they would have responded to our suggestions.

What is your opinion on this claim? And what is the Shī'ī belief regarding creational guardianship? Does it mean that Ahl al-Bayt ﷺ is an active cause in creation and sustenance and is granted such power by God ﷻ – thus avoiding delegation – or

[3] Sūrat al-A'rāf, Verse 188.

does it mean that the Infallible ﷺ manages the universe willfully and voluntarily – as with his other affairs – after being granted such power by God ﷻ or does it mean that the Infallible's ﷺ hand has the potential to receive miraculous capacities when the general interest requires it?

Answer:

In the name of God ﷻ.

The meaning behind creational guardianship is that the guardian's self has reached a perfection level allowing it to manage creational affairs with the permission of God ﷻ and not independently.

This is manifested in the blessed verse

﴿وَأُبرِئُ الأَكْمَهَ وَالأَبرَصَ وَأُحيِي المَوتَىٰ بِإِذنِ اللَّهِ﴾

﴾wa-ʾubriʾu l-ʾakmaha wa-l-ʾabraṣa wa-ʾuḥyi l-mawtā bi-ʾidhni llāhi﴿

﴾And I heal the blind and the leper and I revive the dead by God's leave﴿[4]

[4] Sūrat Āl ʿImrān, Verse 49.

And the verse

﴿أَنا آتيكَ بِهِ قَبلَ أَن يَرتَدَّ إِلَيكَ طَرفُكَ﴾

﴿*'ana 'ātīka bihī qabla 'an yartadda 'ilayka ṭarfuka*﴾

﴿*'I will bring it to you in the twinkling of an eye'*﴾[5]

Where he directly ascribed the action to himself.

Moreover, the intended meaning behind the term 'permission' in the verse is creational permission, that is, the power granted by God ﷻ rather than a sort of legislative permission.

As for the negating verses such as:

﴿قُل لا أَملِكُ لِنَفسي نَفعًا وَلا ضَرًّا إِلّا ما شاءَ اللَّهُ﴾

﴿*qul lā 'amliku li-nafsī naf'an wa-lā ḍarran 'illā mā shā'a llāhu*﴾

[5] Sūrat al-Naml, Verse 40.

﴾Say, *'I have no control over any benefit for myself nor [over] any harm except what God may wish'*﴿[6]

They intend to denounce the idea of independent behavior and not the guardianship granted by God ﷻ.

In addition to the above, the Friends of God عليهم السلام do not manage creational affairs in response to every suggestion they receive. Instead, they manage these affairs in situations where God's ﷻ wisdom demands it from them to preserve the interests of legislation and creation.

In conclusion, based on the description mentioned above, creational guardianship is of the explicit theologies that do not leave any doubt for a person who reflects on the verses and observes the condition of the prophets and Imāms عليهم السلام as mentioned in ḥadīths and narrations. And God ﷻ is the One Who guides towards the straight path.

[6] Sūrat al-Aʿrāf, Verse 188.

The Limits of Exaggeration (*Mughālāt*)

Question 3:

What is the limit for exaggeration? And is a man's belief system considered to be righteous if he believes that the Imāms ؑ has a position that is not reached by the angels that are close to God ﷻ or even by any sent prophet, or if he believes in the content of the grand Ziyārat Jāmiʿah? Does the cursing in the verse

﴿يَدُ اللَّهِ مَغْلُولَةٌ ۚ غُلَّت أَيدِيهِم وَلُعِنوا بِما قالوا ۘ بَل يَداهُ مَبسوطَتانِ﴾

⟨*yadu llāhi maghlūlatun ghullat ʾaydīhim wa-luʿinū bi-mā qālū bal yadāhu mabsūṭatāni*⟩

⟨*'God's hand is tied up.' Tied up be their hands, and cursed be they for what they say! Rather, His hands are wide open*⟩[7]

Include those who say that God has delegated to the Imāms ؑ the religious rulings and affairs related to creation and sustenance, given that they

---

[7] Sūrat al-Māʾidah, Verse 64.

admit and submit to the fact that all of the above is from God ﷻ – such that He is the One who granted and delegated to them these powers whereby they carry out the process of creating all creatures, managing their sustenance, making clouds poor in the rain and plants flourish with fruits, just as Azrael captures the souls?

Answer:

In the name of God ﷻ.

We believe the Prophet and Imāms ﷺ are all intermediaries between God ﷻ and His creations. This great position means that God's ﷻ bounties reach His ﷻ servants, and evils are averted through their blessings. God ﷻ says:

﴿وَابتَغوا إِلَيهِ الوَسيلَةَ﴾

﴿*wa-btaghū 'ilayhi l-wasīlata*﴾

﴿*And seek the means of recourse to Him*﴾[8]

The exaggerators are those who exaggerate how they view the Prophet and Imāms ﷺ such that it

[8] Sūrat al-Mā'idah, Verse 35.

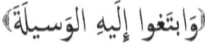

no longer matches our beliefs and perception of them. An example of such exaggeration would be when they claimed that the Prophet and Imāms ؏ are associates of God ﷻ in worship, creation, and sustenance, or that God ﷻ is embodied in them, or that they know about the Unseen without revelation or divine inspiration, or that they are all prophets, or that their souls are all duplicated, or that knowing them makes one needless of fulfilling other obligations, or other false claims of its likes.

Based on the above, believing that the Imāms have a position not reached by a close angel or a sent prophet – except for our Prophet Muḥammad ﷺ – or believing in the meanings within the grant Ziyārat Jāmiʿah is correct and aligned with faith.

As for the Verse

﴿يَدُ اللَّهِ مَغْلُولَةٌ ۚ غُلَّتْ أَيْدِيهِم﴾

⟨*yadu llāhi maghlūlatun ghullat ʾaydīhim*⟩

⟨*'God's hand is tied up.' Tied up be their hands*⟩[9]

---

[9] Sūrat al-Māʾidah, Verse 64.

It addresses the Jews due to their denial of God's ﷻ power of managing affairs and the concept of al-Badā' (change in Divine Will and Decree). This Verse does not tackle the topic of our discussion. It does not address creational guardianship, which is the creational management of all creatures – including people and others – and implied in several verses such as the following:

﴿وَأَوحَينا إِلىٰ موسىٰ أَن أَلقِ عَصاكَ ۖ فَإِذا هِيَ تَلقَفُ ما يَأفِكونَ﴾

﴿*wa-'awḥaynā 'ilā mūsā 'an 'alqi 'aṣāka fa-'idhā hiya talqafu mā ya'fikūna*﴾

﴿فَوَقَعَ الحَقُّ وَبَطَلَ ما كانوا يَعمَلونَ﴾

﴿*fa-waqa'a l-ḥaqqu wa-baṭala mā kānū ya'malūna*﴾

﴿*And We signaled to Moses: 'Throw down your staff.' And behold, it was swallowing what they had faked. So the truth came out, and what they had wrought was reduced to naught*﴾[10]

[10] Sūrat al-A'rāf, Verse 117-118.

And His saying:

﴿إذ قالَ اللَّهُ يا عيسَى ابنَ مَريَمَ اذكُر نِعمَتي عَلَيكَ وَعَلىٰ
والِدَتِكَ إذ أَيَّدتُكَ بِروحِ القُدُسِ تُكَلِّمُ النّاسَ فِي المَهدِ وَكَهلًا ۖ
وَإذ عَلَّمتُكَ الكِتابَ وَالحِكمَةَ وَالتَّوراةَ وَالإنجيلَ ۖ وَإذ تَخلُقُ مِنَ
الطّينِ كَهَيئَةِ الطَّيرِ بِإذني فَتَنفُخُ فيها فَتَكونُ طَيرًا بِإذني ۖ وَتُبرِئُ
الأَكمَهَ وَالأَبرَصَ بِإذني ۖ وَإذ تُخرِجُ المَوتىٰ بِإذني﴾

﴿ʾidh qāla llāhu yā-ʿīsā bna maryama dhkur niʿmatī ʿalayka wa-ʿalā wālidatika ʾidh ʾayyadtuka bi-rūḥi l-qudusi tukallimu n-nāsa fī l-mahdi wa-kahlan wa-ʾidh ʿallamtuka l-kitāba wa-l-ḥikmata wa-t-tawrāta wa-l-ʾinjīla wa-ʾidh takhluqu mina ṭ-ṭīni ka-hayʾati ṭ-ṭayri bi-ʾidhnī fa-tanfukhu fīhā fa-takūnu ṭayran bi-ʾidhnī wa-tubriʾu l-ʾakmaha wa-l-ʾabraṣa bi-ʾidhnī wa-ʾidh tukhriju l-mawtā bi-ʾidhnī﴾

﴿When God will say, O Jesus son of Mary, remember My blessing upon you and upon your mother, when I strengthened you with the Holy Spirit, so you would speak to the people in the cradle and in adulthood, and when I taught you the Book and wisdom, the Torah and the Evangel, and when you would create from clay the form of a bird, with My leave, and you would breathe into it and it would become a bird,

with My leave; and you would heal the blind and the leper, with My leave, and you would raise the dead, with My leave﴿[11]

Amongst other verses where God ﷻ attributed actions to the prophets.

And since it is not possible that this attribute is given to the prophets while excluding our Prophet ﷺ, then it applies to our Prophet Muḥammad ﷺ as well. And since Imām Alī b. Abī Ṭālib ؑ is proven to be the Prophet's self ﷺ by Qur'ānic proof, and since there is not any difference between the Imāms ؑ, then what applies to the prophets applies to the Prophet ﷺ and consequently to the Imāms ؑ except for the position of prophethood.

The difference between the Prophets and the Imāms ؑ is that the former used to do that to prove their prophethood through miracles. As for the Imāms ؑ, they generally refrained from doing this except in rare situations, as mentioned in the narrations. And people were obligated to know them, as a trial conducted by God with the nation after the death of the Messenger ﷺ in pursuit of

[11] Sūrat al-Mā'idah, Verse 110.

distinguishing those who follow his words ﷺ from those who do not. Moreover, it has been narrated in Ziyārat al-Jāmiʿah that they are the door with whom people are tested. How, then, does one believe and commit to their Imāmate and to the fact that they are the equal of the Prophet ﷺ except in Prophethood, yet refrain from doing so in regards to their creational guardianship, even though wisdom demands that creational guardianship falls in their hands so they can nullify the statements of those who claim Prophethood after the Prophet ﷺ through sorcery and other ways that harm people?

And God is the All-Knowing.

Infallibility

Question 4:

Some authors say that God's ﷻ saying:

﴿وَلَقَدْ هَمَّتْ بِهِۦ وَهَمَّ بِهَا لَوْلَا أَن رَّأَىٰ بُرْهَانَ رَبِّهِۦ﴾

﴾*wa-la-qad hammat bihī wa-hamma bihā law-lā ʾan raʾā burhāna rabbihī*﴿

﴾She certainly made for him; and he would have made for her [too] had he not beheld the proof of his Lord﴿[12]

means that: "Yūsuf ﷺ moved according to his desires – his human sexual instincts – towards the action after being seduced; however, when he saw his Lord's proof, he refrained from sinning." And there is no proof that this extent of having the urge to sin does not exist in the infallible person. That which negates infallibility is the external sin.

What is the Shīʿī belief concerning infallibility and its scope?

Answer:

In the name of God ﷻ.

The intended meaning behind infallibility is that Prophets and Imāms ﷺ reached a level of knowledge and certainty that eliminated from within themselves the urge to sin – let alone actually committing them. And this does not contradict man's ability to sin. Moreover, the ordinary man has a degree of infallibility in

---

[12] Sūrat Yūsuf, Verse 24.

committing certain atrocious actions, such as eating dirt, while maintaining the capacity to do so. However, due to its extreme hideousness in his eyes, the urge to commit this action does not kindle in him – let alone actually commit it.

God ﷻ gave the Prophets and Imāms ﷺ this unique characteristic due to His ﷻ knowledge that they have distinguished themselves from the rest of mankind due to their strong obedience to God ﷻ, regardless of this characteristic. And this does not negate their capacity to sin, as previously mentioned.

As for the verse resorted to in the above question as evidence, it can instead be used as evidence against the claim intended. The phrase 'had it not been for' implies his refraining from sinning due to seeing his Lord's ﷻ proof.

This is the theological belief of the Shīʿa, which is based on Qurʾānic verses and narrations, especially the Verse of Purification that addressed the infallibility of Ahl al-Bayt ﷺ. And every statement that negates what we mentioned is considered to be in opposition to the beliefs of the Shīʿī sect.

Question 5:

What is the opinion of the Shīʿa scholars in regards to the following statement that comments on the verse:

﴿قَالَ رَبِّ اغفِر لي وَلِأَخي﴾

﴿qāla rabbi ghfir lī wa-li-ʾakhī﴾

﴿He said, 'My Lord, forgive me and my brother'﴾[13]

and what is the ruling regarding the person who believes in it? The statement is as follows: "However, we do not find such issues harmful to the position of infallibility; as we do not perceive the principle in a metaphysical way that prevents man from such mistakes in evaluating things. Instead, the concern is not to disobey God by engaging in actions that one knows to be sinful. As for the claim that he does not commit a wrongful act which he believes is righteous and legitimate, we do not find any proof that upholds such a claim. We rather notice, in this regard, that the Qurʾānic approach in speaking about the life of the prophets and their weaknesses emphasizes the claim that

[13] Sūrat al-Aʿrāf, Verse 151.

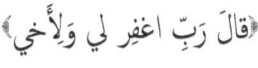

Prophethood (or being a carrier of the divine message) does not contradict with having some human weaknesses such as making mistakes when it comes to evaluating certain things."

Answer:

In the name of God ﷻ.

Misevaluating certain things while assuming that the evaluation is correct is not a sin that requires a request for forgiveness. And the blessed verse explicitly mentioned the request for forgiveness, which implies that the subject is unrelated to a mistake in evaluation or judgment. Instead, it is related to a particular behavior that is not appropriate for the position of a prophet, such as Prophet Yūnus's ؑ escape from his people – even though it does not form disobedience of a prohibition imposed by God ﷻ which necessitates a request for forgiveness – which is based on the premise that "the good deeds performed by virtuous individuals are considered misdeeds when performed by those who have attained further proximity to God ﷻ. In regards to what is mentioned in the question, it is indeed false; for if we legitimize error in evaluation and judgment on behalf of the prophet, then his commands and prohibitions will no longer be trusted due to the possibility of fallibility in giving commands on behalf of God ﷻ which in reality do not match the actual command.

The space given in this document only allows for further details.

And God ﷻ is the All-Knowing.

The Infallibility of Prophets

Question 6:

What is your opinion regarding those who make the following claims about the prophets' infallibility? And what is the legal ruling regarding their theological belief? The claim is as follows: It is possible, on an abstract level, for a prophet to make a mistake while informing others of a specific verse or to forget about it entirely at some point, only to repair the mistake later on until the verse is fully and correctly communicated.

The individual who made a claim above also objected to 'Allamah Sayyid Muḥammad Ḥusayn Ṭabāṭabā'ī's words on the Prophet's ﷺ infallibility in regards to passing the divine message which "does not get fulfilled except with the infallibility of the Prophet from sinning and his protectiveness from committing any violation"[14]. The individual who objected to the Allamah said: However, the human action may emerge based on the practical reality which may move within him through his circumstances that are subjected to some occurring whimsies due to internal or external pressures, whether sensual or spiritual, whereby the person may retreat from it to uphold the principle which he has shown to people from the standpoint of revelation. This is just like the case of the reformers and carriers of divine messages – even the pious amongst them – who may deviate in their practical steps away from the path of revelation.

Answer:

In the name of God ﷻ.

---

[14] Ṭabāṭabā'ī, 'Allamah Sayyid Muḥammad Ḥusayn, *al-Mīzān fī Tafsīr al-Qur'ān,* Vol. 2, p. 137, new edition.

If the Prophet's ﷺ fallibility in disseminating a verse or forgetting it is possible, then it will be similarly possible for him to fall into error when correcting it afterward. This, then, demands the invalidation of Prophethood which requires infallibility as pointed out in the verse:

﴿وَما يَنطِقُ عَنِ الهَوىٰ﴾

﴿wa-mā yanṭiqu ʿani l-hawā﴾

﴿إِن هُوَ إِلّا وَحيٌ يوحىٰ﴾

﴿ʾin huwa ʾillā waḥyun yūḥā﴾

﴿Nor does he speak out of [his own] desire: it is just a revelation that is revealed [to him]﴾[15]

As for the second part of the statement, it is false. For, the infallibility of the Prophet ﷺ demands that he does not carry out any action unless it matches the religious obligation and that he does not give any command or impose any prohibition unless it matches revelation.

[15] Sūrat al-Najm, Verse 3-4.

This has been manifested in the blessed verse:

﴿وَلَو تَقَوَّلَ عَلَينا بَعضَ الأَقاويلِ﴾

﴿*wa-law taqawwala ʿalaynā baʿḍa l-ʾaqāwīl*[i]﴾

﴿لَأَخَذنا مِنهُ بِاليَمينِ﴾

﴿*la-ʾakhadhnā minhu bi-l-yamīn*[i]﴾

﴿ثُمَّ لَقَطَعنا مِنهُ الوَتينَ﴾

﴿*thumma la-qaṭaʿnā minhu l-watīn*[a]﴾

﴿*Had he faked any sayings in Our name, We would have surely seized him by the right hand and then cut off his aorta*﴾[16]

In conclusion, this statement goes against the Shīʿī theological belief.

[16] Sūrat al-Ḥāqqah, Verses 44-46.

The Personality of Sayyidah Fāṭimah al-Zahrā' ﷺ and the Four Women

Question 7:

What is your opinion about those who say the following about Sayyidah Fāṭimah al-Zahrā' ﷺ and the nature of her blessed character – in addition to Sayyidah Zaynab, Khadījah al-Kubra, Maryam and the wife of Pharaoh ﷺ? The statement is as follows: "Some people say that these women acquire some unusual characteristics; however, we do not see that there is a special feature therein besides the natural circumstances that allowed them to grow on a spiritual and intellectual level and to maintain practical commitment at the level where the elements of their personalities attained balance naturally along the journey of personal development. And we cannot resort to the ḥadīth that mentions the presence of special unseen elements that distinguish them from ordinary women; no conclusive evidence upholds it."

Answer:

In the name of God ﷻ.

This statement is false in its entirety – starting from its premises. For, the creation of Sayyidah Fāṭimah al-Zahrā' عليها السلام - as the creation of the Imāms عليهم السلام – took place through God's ﷻ special grace due to His ﷻ knowledge that they would worship God ﷻ and obey Him ﷻ with utmost sincerity. Moreover, it is not strange for the Friends of God to be given special characteristics that distinguish them from others upon creation. And the Noble Qur'ān testifies for this regarding Prophet ʿĪsā ibn Maryam عليه السلام. Furthermore, it has been mentioned in many narrations which have correct chains of ḥadīth (sanad Ṣaḥīḥ) - and which were mentioned by the elite and the public – that Sayyidah Fāṭimah al-Zahrā' عليها السلام was privileged in having the drop of seminal fluid – through which she was conceived – created from the fruits of Heaven. In addition, it was mentioned in the narrations that she used to communicate with her mother, Sayyidah Khadījah عليها السلام when she was a fetus in her womb. It was also mentioned that angels used to descend upon her. For, it was narrated in Ṣaḥīḥ Abi Obeida that Imām Jaʿfar al-Ṣādiq عليه السلام said that Fāṭimah عليها السلام lived for seventy-five days after the death of her father ﷺ. She was utterly grieved for the loss of her father ﷺ that the angel Gabriel used to descend upon her to console and relieve her by telling her about her father ﷺ, his position, and the descendants that would emerge from her. And Imām Alī b. Abī Ṭālib ‫عليه السلام‬ would write all of that down.

Moreover, the oppression she underwent was frequently narrated and, therefore, does not need proof to uphold it. Nonetheless, the fact that she was buried at night and that her grave has been concealed until this very day is sufficient proof of her oppression. And all that is written in denial of her unique characteristics regarding her creation and denial of her oppression is considered among the books that deviate people from the straight path.

Infallibility: Compulsory or Optional

Question 8:

What is your opinion regarding those who object to Shaykh Muḥammad b. Muḥammad b. Nuʿmān Mufīd's claim that infallibility is optional and adopts the claim that it is mandatory whereby they say the following: "The approach which claims that infallibility is optional while adopting the belief that God establishes it as He creates His Prophet or Friend, only represents an understanding that stems from the proof which combines the mandatory nature of infallibility and the necessity of optionality, rather than an accurate study of the quality of the realistic picture which combines both."

Then they say: "We inquire about the reason that prevented God from choosing some of His servants to be infallible, given that people need them. What could the problem be, especially that His servants' interests would be secured? If the issue lies in their entitlement to a reward for actions they did not choose, then the response to this would be the following: If the reward given to man for his obedience to God is out of God's mere bountifulness rather than man's entitlement to this reward, then why wouldn't God bestow His bounties upon man directly? There is nothing wicked about rewarding someone for an action they did not choose; rather, the wickedness lies in punishing someone for doing something he cannot help but do."

Then, they say: "The contemporary interpretational studies and other types of studies started to interpret the verses that explicitly mention the prophets' sinful acts in a way that does not negate their infallibility. However, the question to be raised here is the following: What is the reason for having the Qur'ānic approach in speaking about the prophets in a way that negates the concept of infallibility? And what is the scope within which interpretation can move – given the accuracy and eloquence of the verses? One of the problems identified in many interpretational approaches that go beyond the explicit meaning of the Verse is that they reach a level where the words lose their accuracy completely, which contradicts the miraculous characteristic of the Noble Qur'ān."

Answer:

In the name of God ﷻ.

The essay above tackles three issues:

The First Issue: It is related to the reality of infallibility.

The answer to this issue is as follows: According to the school that believes in the Imāmate of the Imāms (also called the Imamiyyah), infallibility means that the Imām or Prophet ﷺ reaches a high level of knowledge and certainly with which the will or desire to sin no longer kindles within himself, despite his ability to sin. And this is a possible and realistic situation. Many people have a certain extent of infallibility regarding hideous actions considered inappropriate, such as walking in the street naked. An honorable man has a certain level of infallibility that prevents him from committing such a hideous act; that is, despite his ability to commit such an act, the desire or willingness to do so does not kindle inside him.

As for the second issue, which is related to the optionality of infallibility, the answer to it is as follows:

It is impossible to claim that infallibility is imposed involuntarily on the Infallible عليه السلام; otherwise, his obligation in terms of commandments and prohibitions would be invalid as it would constitute an imposition of an obligation that exceeds one's capacities, knowing that it is well-established and necessary that the Infallibles عليهم السلام have such obligations. This is emphasized in the following Qur'ānic verse:

﴿لَئِنْ أَشْرَكْتَ لَيَحْبَطَنَّ عَمَلُكَ وَلَتَكُونَنَّ مِنَ الْخَاسِرِينَ﴾

﴿*la-'in 'ashrakta la-yaḥbaṭanna 'amaluka wa-la-takūnanna mina l-khāsirīna*﴾

﴿*'If you ascribe a partner to God your works shall fail and you shall surely be among the losers*﴾[17]

And similar verses, in addition to the fact that if obedience has been imposed involuntarily upon the Imam, he would not be an excellent example to be followed by the people – which negates the necessities of religion and the Shī'ī beliefs. This is indicated in verse:

﴿لَقَدۡ كَانَ لَكُمۡ فِي رَسُولِ ٱللَّهِ أُسۡوَةٌ حَسَنَةٌ﴾

﴿*la-qad kāna lakum fī rasūli llāhi 'uswatun ḥasanatun*﴾

﴿*In the Apostle of God there is certainly for you a good exemplar*﴾[18]

and in Imām Alī b. Abī Ṭālib's saying: "Indeed, every follower has an Imām whom he can follow and get enlightened by the luminosity of his

---

[17] Sūrat al-Zumar, Verse 65.

[18] Sūrat al-Aḥzāb, Verse 21.

knowledge. Indeed, your Imām was satisfied with his two old ragged clothes...."

As for the third issue, which is related to the Qur'ānic verses that contradict the concept of infallibility, the answer to this claim is as follows:

Every Qur'ānic verse with rational proof that negates its exterior is interpreted according to that proof. This has been the practice of rational scholars in such situations. Any words from a wise person – let alone God's – cannot be interpreted according to their exoteric meaning independently of rational and necessary provisions, focused proofs, and customs. Thus, what has been mentioned by our virtuous scholars in regards to the clarification of the Qur'ānic verses – as done by Sayyid al-Murtaḍa 'Alam al-Huda' in his book Tanzīh al-Anbiyā' – does not negate the eloquence of the verses; it is rather quite harmonious with the similes and figures of speech. Such expressions are based on the premise that "the good deeds performed by virtuous individuals are considered misdeeds when performed by those who have attained further proximity to God ﷻ."

And God is the All-Knowing.

The Verse: The Prophet Frowned and Turned Away

Question 9:

What is your opinion on those who say that the Verse:

﴿عَبَسَ وَتَوَلَّىٰ﴾

﴾*'abasa wa-tawallā*﴿

﴾*He frowned and turned away*﴿[19]

was addressing the frown of the Messenger ﷺ and his turning away at the arrival of 'Abdullah b. Umm Maktūm?

Answer:

In the name of God ﷻ.

It was narrated that the Imāms عليهم السلام mentioned that this verse was revealed in regards to a man who was sitting in a gathering with the Prophet ﷺ, and that verse was a form of reproach and blame for that

[19] Sūrat 'Abasa, Verse 1.

man who was present in the Prophet's gathering. This is verified by the verse's inclusion of content that does not match the Qur'ānic description of the Prophet's ﷺ personality. For example, God ﷻ says:

﴿أَمَّا مَنِ اسْتَغْنَىٰ﴾

﴿'ammā mani staghnā﴾

﴿فَأَنتَ لَهُ تَصَدَّىٰ﴾

﴿fa-'anta lahū taṣaddā﴾

﴿وَمَا عَلَيْكَ أَلَّا يَزَّكَّىٰ﴾

﴿wa-mā 'alayka 'allā yazzakkā﴾

﴿But as for someone who is self-complacent, you attend to him, though you are not liable if he does not purify himself﴾[20]

Which is clear that the person addressed by this verse has the habit of attending to wealthy people and neglecting their purification and refinement. And this opposes what God ﷻ said regarding the Prophet ﷺ:

---

[20] Sūrat 'Abasa, Verses 5-7.

﴿هُوَ الَّذِي بَعَثَ فِي الأُمِّيِّينَ رَسولًا مِنهُم يَتلو عَلَيهِم آياتِهِ وَيُزَكّيهِم وَيُعَلِّمُهُمُ الكِتابَ وَالحِكمَةَ وَإِن كانوا مِن قَبلُ لَفي ضَلالٍ مُبينٍ﴾

﴿huwa lladhī baʿatha fī l-ʾummiyyīna rasūlan minhum yatlū ʿalayhim ʾāyātihī wa-yuzakkīhim wa-yuʿallimuhumu l-kitāba wa-l-ḥikmata wa-ʾin kānū min qablu la-fī ḍalālin mubīnin﴾

﴿It is He who sent to the unlettered [people] an apostle from among themselves, to recite to them His signs, to purify them, and to teach them the Book and wisdom, and earlier they had indeed been in manifest error﴾[21]

And

﴿وَأَمّا مَن جاءَكَ يَسعىٰ﴾

﴿wa-ʾammā man jāʾaka yasʿā﴾

﴿وَهُوَ يَخشىٰ﴾

﴿wa-huwa yakhshā﴾

﴿فَأَنتَ عَنهُ تَلَهّىٰ﴾

---

[21] Sūrat al-Jumuʿah, Verse 2.

﴾*fa-'anta 'anhu talahhā*﴿

﴾*But he who comes hurrying to you, while he fears [God], you are neglectful of him*﴿[22]

It is clear from the verses above that the addressed person has the habit of neglecting believers, which opposes God's speech about the Prophet ﷺ when He said:

﴿لَقَد جاءَكُم رَسولٌ مِن أَنفُسِكُم عَزيزٌ عَلَيهِ ما عَنِتُّم حَريصٌ عَلَيكُم بِالمُؤمِنينَ رَءوفٌ رَحيمٌ﴾

﴾*la-qad jā'akum rasūlun min 'anfusikum 'azīzun 'alayhi mā 'anittum ḥarīṣun 'alaykum bi-l-mu'minīna ra'ūfun raḥīm^un^*﴿

﴾*There has certainly come to you an apostle from among yourselves. Grievous to him is your distress; he has deep concern for you, and is most kind and merciful to the faithful*﴿[23]

In fact, the claim that the Prophet carried out this sort of behavior ﷺ necessitates the attribution of

---

[22] Sūrat 'Abasa, Verses 8-10.

[23] Sūrat al-Tawbah, Verse 128.

disobedience to the Prophet ﷺ, as he has the obligation of welcoming believers and humbling himself for them, which is mentioned in His saying:

﴿وَاخفِض جَناحَكَ لِلمُؤمِنينَ﴾

﴿*wa-khfiḍ janāḥaka li-l-mu’minīn*[a]﴾

﴿*and lower* your *wing to the faithful**﴾[24]

The Infallibility of People Other than Prophets and Imāms عليهم السلام

Question 10:

Is it proper to claim that people besides Prophets and Imāms عليهم السلام are infallible, such as Sayyidah Zaynab عليها السلام and Abī al-Faḍl al-‘Abbās عليه السلام? Does infallibility come in different levels?

---

[24] Sūrat al-Ḥijr, Verse 88.

* That is, be humble and gracious towards them. Cf. 17:24; 26:215.

Answer:

In the name of God ﷻ.

The infallibility mentioned by God ﷻ in the Verse of Purification is specific to the Prophet ﷺ, Sayyidah Fāṭimah al-Zahrā' and the Imāms ﷺ – who is referred to as the fourteen Infallibles ﷺ. Therefore, the other individuals who relate and belong to the Prophet ﷺ or pure Imāms ﷺ do not have this specific type of infallibility. Nonetheless, they can acquire a lower level of infallibility which still distinguishes them from the rest of the pious and virtuous people, as is the case with Abī al-Faḍl al-'Abbās, Sayyidah Zaynab ﷺ and others whose rights and positions were mentioned in ḥadīths narrated on behalf of the Infallibles ﷺ.

Her patience, tolerance, great stances, speeches that were described in the narrations as if they were spoken by [...], and other well-known and frequently narrated characteristics established within us a sense of security which enabled us to claim that she reached a high level of purity which distinguished her from other women. The same applies to Abī al-Faḍl al-'Abbās ﷺ, his altruism towards his brother al-Ḥusayn ﷺ, and his tolerance of calamities for the sake of religion and the flourishing of the Shīʿī School of Thought – which is well known amongst the general Muslims let alone the believers.

And God is All-Knowing.

The Light of the Infallibles عليهم السلام

Question 11:

Some authors raised doubts in regards to the following saying: "The Prophet's household, including Sayyidah Fāṭimah al-Zahrāʾ عليها السلام, were created as lights before the creation of existence." And it was mentioned that such narrations' chain of transmission was considered weak.

What is your opinion on this matter? Is it amongst the matters upon which there is consensus within the Shīʿī circle or amongst the popular and well-established matters within credible narrations?

Answer:

In the name of God عز وجل.

It has been mentioned in many narrations that God ﷻ created the light of Sayyidah Fāṭimah al-Zahrāʾ ؑ from His light before the creation of Ādam ؑ. These narrations can neither be claimed as lies nor be denounced. Moreover, it has been recalled in Maʿānī al-ʾAkhbār, with a correct chain of transmission, that Sadeer recalled that Imām Jaʿfar al-Ṣādiq ؑ[25] confirmed the truthfulness of this matter.

Although believing in this matter is not a religious duty or a necessity according to the Shīʿī School of Thought, it is still a factor that perfects one's beliefs. Whoever acquires such beliefs from their correct sources – with certainty and assurance – is considered to have achieved great success.

The Light of Sayyidah Fāṭimah al-Zahrāʾ ؑ

Question 12:

Some raised doubts regarding the narrations that mentioned that the light of Sayyidah Fāṭimah al-Zahrāʾ ؑ had been created before God ﷻ created the Earth and sky. What is your opinion on that

---

[25] Ṣadūq, Shaykh Muḥammad b. ʿAlī, *Maʿānī al-ʾAkhbār*, p. 396, ḥadīth 53.

matter, knowing that being strict regarding the authenticity of the chain of transmission does not exclude some narrations from the circle of credibility? For we see this manifested in the narration of Sadir al-Sayrafi[26], which is mentioned by Shaykh Muḥammad b. ʿAlī (Ibn Bābawayh) Ṣadūq in Maʿānī al-ʾAkhbār.

Answer:

In the name of God ﷻ.

It has been mentioned in some narrations – amongst which were credible ones – that the Prophet ﷺ and his Infallible progeny عليهم السلام – amongst whom was Sayyidah Fāṭimah al-Zahrāʾ عليها السلام – were present with their luminous shadows before the creation of Ādam عليه السلام; and their materialistic creation came later than Ādam's عليه السلام creation – which is quite clear.

And God is the All-Knowing.

[26] Ṣadūq, Shaykh Muḥammad b. ʿAlī, *Maʿānī al-ʾAkhbār*, p. 396, chapter of *Nawadir al-Maʿānī*.

The Book of Fāṭimah ؑ

Question 13:

Some authors mentioned that: Sayyidah Fāṭimah al-Zahrāʾ ؑ was the first author of Islam; for she used to write what she heard from her father al-Muṣṭafā ﷺ regarding rulings and teachings. She compiled all her writings in the "Book of Fāṭimah".

What do you think about this saying? Does it agree with the Shīʿī belief in "the Book of Fāṭimah?"

Answer:

In the name of God ﷻ.

What is meant by the "Book of Fāṭimah" is mentioned in authentic narrations in al-Kāfī, such as the following: "One of the angels used to descend upon Sayyidah Fāṭimah al-Zahrāʾ ؑ after the death of her father ﷺ, console her and reveal to her of what will unfold in the future; and Imām Alī b. Abī Ṭālib ؑ used to write what was being told – which was later called the "Book of Fāṭimah".[27]

---

[27] Kulaynī, Shaykh Muḥammad b. Yaʿqūb, *al-Kāfī,* Vol. 1 p. 240, ḥadīth 2, and p. 241, ḥadīth 5.

Accordingly, it is not a Qur'ān as the enemies of the Shī'a imagined or claimed falsely. And it is not a book that comprises rulings – as mentioned in the question; it is rather odd and opposing to authentic narrations. Moreover, there is nothing bizarre about the conversation between Sayyidah Fāṭimah al-Zahrā' ﷺ and the angels; for the Noble Qur'ān mentioned that the angels conversed with Sayyidah Maryam ﷺ, the daughter of Imran:

﴿وَإِذ قالَتِ المَلائِكَةُ يا مَريَمُ إِنَّ اللَّهَ اصطَفاكِ وَطَهَّرَكِ وَاصطَفاكِ عَلى نِساءِ العالَمينَ﴾

﴿wa-'idh qālati l-malā'ikatu yā-maryamu 'inna llāha ṣṭafāki wa-ṭahharaki wa-ṣṭafāki 'alā nisā'i l-'ālamīna﴾

﴿And when the angels said, 'O Mary, God has chosen you and purified you, and He has chosen you above the world's women﴾[28]

And it is well-known amongst us – the Shī'a – that Sayyidah Fāṭimah al-Zahrā' ﷺ has a higher position than Sayyidah Maryam ﷺ, daughter of Imran. Furthermore, it was mentioned in the authentic

---

[28] Sūrat Āl 'Imrān, Verse 42.

narrations that Sayyidah Maryam عليها السلام was the Lady of the women of her age and that Sayyidah Fāṭimah al-Zahrā' was the Lady of the Women of all Worlds.

The Tragedies of Sayyidah Fāṭimah al-Zahrā' عليها السلام

Question 14:

Some authors say: Some narrations that mention the tragedies of Sayyidah Fāṭimah al-Zahrā' عليها السلام are not accurate, for I do not think that Sayyidah Fāṭimah al-Zahrā' عليها السلام had anything better to do during her days and nights than weeping. And I do not think that Sayyidah Fāṭimah al-Zahrā' عليها السلام used to weep until the people in her city got annoyed by her weeping, despite her understanding of God's ﷻ divine decree and destiny and the fact that patience is of the required Islamic values even if the deceased was someone in the position of the Messenger of God ﷺ.

Is the excessive weeping of Sayyidah Fāṭimah al-Zahrā ' عليها السلام and Imām Zayn al-ʿĀbidīn عليه السلام certain according to the Shīʿī beliefs?

Was her weeping purely emotional, or was it a role fulfilled by one of the Infallibles ﷺ in pursuit of achieving specific goals? In case it was purely emotional, does it contradict surrendering to God's ﷻ Divine Decree and Destiny, especially since the deceased is al-Muṣṭafā ﷺ?

Answer:

In the name of God ﷻ.

The intended meaning behind the weeping of Sayyidah Fāṭimah al-Zahrā' ﷺ during the day and night times is not that her weeping occupied her entire day and night; it instead means that her weeping used to occur at different times and is not specific to a particular time during the day. Moreover, weeping as an expression of mercy and sympathy does not negate patience during calamities and surrendering to God's ﷻ divine decree and destiny. For, the Prophet Yaʿqūb ﷺ wept for his separation from his son Yūsuf ﷺ until his eyes became blind out of sorrow – as mentioned in the Noble Qur'ān – even though he was an infallible prophet.

Furthermore, the weeping of Sayyidah Fāṭimah al-Zahrā' over her father was, on the one hand, emotional due to her loss of her father al-Muṣṭafā and, on the other hand, a manifestation of her oppression and the oppression of her husband, a form of shedding light on the usurpation of Amīr al-Mu'minīn's right to the Islamic caliphate and an expression of sadness for the Muslims due to the reversion of some of them as mentioned by the blessed verse:

﴿أَفَإِن ماتَ أَو قُتِلَ انقَلَبتُم عَلَى أَعقابِكُم﴾

'a-fa-'in māta 'aw qutila nqalabtum 'alā
'a'qābikum

⟨If he dies or is slain, will you turn back on your heels?⟩[29]

How, then, is she expected not to weep after seeing all the efforts of the Messenger of God going down the drain regarding the upbringing and nurturing of some Muslims.

Moreover, weeping over the tragedy of Imām al-Ḥusayn is considered to be one of the

---

[29] Sūrat Āl 'Imrān, Verse 144.

sacraments of God ﷻ; as it is a manifestation of righteousness for which Imām al-Ḥusayn ؑ sacrificed himself and a denial of falsehood which the Umayyads manifested. That was the reason for which Imām Zayn al-ʿĀbidīn ؑ wept for an extended period over his father, as a manifestation of the oppression suffered by Imām al-Ḥusayn ؑ and as a triumph of his objectives and aims.

It is well-established by the Imāmate Shīʿa that Sayyidah Fāṭimah al-Zahrāʾ ؑ and Imām Zayn al-ʿĀbidīn ؑ wept for quite an extended period.

The Oppression of Sayyidah Fāṭimah al-Zahrāʾ ؑ

Question 15:

What is your opinion regarding the person who says, "I do not feel engaged with several ḥadīths that say that the people broke her ribs or hit her on her face and so on." Then, when this person was asked: "How can we exclude the breaking of Sayyidah Fāṭimah al-Zahrāʾ's ribs, knowing that the word 'even so' was spoken by those who initiated the attack – which ensued the implication. In addition to that, how can we explain the loss of the fetus,

Muḥsin?" He said: "I said: This was not proven by authentic narrations; however, it could be possible. As for the miscarriage of the fetus, it could have happened according to the normal course of things."

Answer:

In the name of God.

The concealment of her grave and she will to be buried at night in pursuit of manifesting the oppression she had suffered sufficient proof of her oppression and the truthfulness of what was narrated regarding the calamities she had endured. This is in addition to the words narrated by Imām Alī b. Abī Ṭālib[30] when he was burying her and on the occasion of her birthday, in the chapter of *al-Ḥujjah*, when he said: "Certainly, your daughter will apprise you of the joining together of your people for the aim of oppressing her. Ask her for the details and get all the news. How many a grudge was clashing within her chest, which she did not find a way to release! But

[30] Kulaynī, Shaykh Muḥammad b. Ya'qūb, *al-Kāfī*, Vol. 1, p. 458.

she will speak; and God will judge. And God is the best of Judges."

He عليه السلام also said: "So in front of God's eyes, your daughter was buried in secret, her rights were usurped, and her inheritance was denied. This had happened when a long time had not elapsed, and your remembrance had not disappeared. To God, I shall raise my complaints."

And in the second part of the same chapter, there is an authentic narration on behalf of Imām Mūsā al-Kāẓim عليه السلام where he عليه السلام said: "Indeed, Fāṭimah is a truthful woman and a martyr." This is well-established through her oppression and martyrdom. This is also supported by the narrations[31] under the proofs of Imāmate by al-Ṭabarī whose narrations are recalled from multiple scholars on behalf of Imām Jaʿfar al-Ṣādiq عليه السلام: "The reason for her death was that Qunfuz was ordered by his master to strike her with the grip of the sword upon which she underwent the miscarriage of Muḥsin."

[31] Majlisī, ʿAllamah Muḥammad Bāqir, *Biḥār al-Anwār*, Vol. 43, ch. 11.

And God is the One who guides towards righteousness.

Ḥusaynī Sacraments

Question 16:

It is mentioned in some sayings that: "Beating one's chest over the tragedies of Imām al-Ḥusayn ﵇ – if done violently in a way that leads to bleeding in the chest or severe pain – is prohibited for different reasons:

1. It is not a civilized way, and the cause of Imām al-Ḥusayn ﵇ must be raised and presented in a realistic and civilized manner.

2. It was not mentioned by the Messenger of God ﷺ and his household ﵈.

3. Harming one's body is prohibited even if it does not lead to death or dismemberment. For, whoever exposes himself to a cold breeze, knowing that this may cause him a disease in his chest, is considered to have committed a prohibited act."

What is your opinion regarding this saying?

Answer:

In the name of God ﷻ.

Beating one's chest as a form of severe sadness for Imām al-Ḥusayn ؑ is considered one of the desired sacraments, as it falls under the title of al-Jazaʿ or desperate impatience. This was pointed out by many authentic narrations, even if it led, in some situations, to bleeding or the darkening of the chest.

Moreover, there is no proof for the prohibition of every act that harms the body as long as it does not reach the level of a crime against one's self, which is considered oppression against one's self. Furthermore, according to their claim, mourning over the tragedy in a civilized manner does not have any relationship with the prohibition or allowing of acts. And God is All-Knowing.

Weeping and Being Impatient

Question 17:

Some declarations mention the following: "There is no need to raise the tragedy of Karbalāʾ; amongst people violently and emotionally whereby a state of emergency and weeping is established. For, this is neither a civilized nor an Islamic approach." What do you think of such a claim?

Answer:

In the name of God ﷻ.

Severe weeping and triggering others to weep are considered desirable acts, and this has been pointed out widely in several narrations. For example, in *al-Wasā'il* (Chapter 66 under the title 'al-Mazār'), there are many narrations that emphasize the desirability of such acts, amongst which is the narration recalled in Ṣaḥīḥ Muʿāwīya b. Wahab, on behalf of Imām Jaʿfar al-Ṣādiq ﷺ, when he asked a Shaykh: "How far are you from the grave of my oppressed grandfather, al-Ḥusayn ?" He said: "I am close to it." He ﷺ said: "How often do you visit him?" He said: "I visit him quite frequently." He ﷺ said: "His blood is that through which God can be invoked." Then he ﷺ said: "All sorts of impatience and weeping are detested, except the impatience and weeping over the murder of Imām al-Ḥusayn ." And God is All-Knowing.

The Cause of Karbalā'

Question 18:

It is said that: "The most authentic resource that narrates the story of Imām al-Ḥusayn 🕮 is the book 'Al-Luhūf 'alā Qatlā al-Tufūf' by Sayyid Ibn Ṭāwūs. What is your opinion on this saying?

Answer:

In the name of God 🕮.

The events of Karbalā' have been verified – in a general manner – in frequently mentioned narrations and authentic ḥadīths recalled on behalf of Ahl al-Bayt 🕮. As for the details of the events, it is sought in several books such as al-Kāfī and books of al-Mazār for our virtuous scholars. The book 'Al-Luhūf' and the book of Abi Mukhnaf are like other history books that undergo scientific research.

And God is All-Knowing.

A False Claim

Question 19:

It has been said in public gatherings that: "Some Shīʿa in Iraq used to drink alcohol on the day of ʿĀshūrāʾ to warm themselves up for the commemoration of the tragedy of ʿĀshūrāʾ.

What are your comments on this saying?

Answer:

In the name of God ﷻ.

This is not true in Iraq or any other Shīʿī country that follows Ahl al-Bayt ﷺ. Whoever spoke those words will be held accountable for them on the Day of Resurrection.

And God is All-Knowing.

Expressions in ʿĀshūrāʾ

Question 20:

It has been mentioned that Sayyid al-Khūʾī established a ruling that considers the well-known expressions of mourning, such as beating chests, as prohibited acts if they cause harm to the image of the Shīʿī creed. What is your comment on that ruling?

Answer:

In the name of God ﷻ.

It has been mentioned earlier that every expression of mourning – if it falls under sadness and impatience with the tragedies of Ahl al-Bayt عليهم السلام – is amongst the desirable acts, especially the unfamiliar practices performed by the Shīʿa to stir up the hearts of people and rouse their emotions in the pursuit of spreading the cause of Imām al-Ḥusayn عليه السلام. This approach of informing and disseminating events has been adopted, even in our current times. Perhaps, those who criticize the practices and mourning expressions of ʿĀshūrāʾ would have remained silent about them had the non-Shīʿa implemented them. And there is neither power nor strength except in God ﷻ.

Doctrinal Necessity

Question 21:

Some writers say the following: "There is a constant and conclusive truth within the Islamic culture, and this has been verified in credible and authentic resources, in terms of chain of transmission and evidence, whereby there is no room left for Ijtihād in this regard (The process by which a scholar extracts the laws of Islam from their four primary sources: the Qur'ān, Sunnah, Consensus, and Intellect.) For, then, Ijtihād would be placed in opposition to the religious designation. This truth is represented in the axiomatic certainties of theological belief, such as belief in monotheism, Prophethood, the Hereafter, and the givens the rise from the Sharī'a, such as the obligatory prayers."

"On the other hand, a variable moves within the world of religious designations subjected to verification and interpretation to Ijtihād. This variable was not clear enough that it reached the level of indisputability, nor was it documented enough to reach the level of indubitable certainty. This variable was the subject of debate amongst Muslims, such as the caliphate, the Imāmate, rational beauty and ugliness which were debated amongst rationalists and others, infallibility in spreading the message and beyond that."

The question is as follows: Is the above saying correct regarding the Imāmate being one of the various issues that have not been verified through conclusive evidence? Is infallibility one of these issues as well?

What is the religious perception of those who adopt such views? Are they considered among the Twelver Imāmate followers, or are they considered among the opposing party? Kindly give us your ruling. May God reward you.

Answer:

In the name of God ﷻ.

The issues of Imamāte and infallibility are amongst the necessities and axioms of the Shīʿī theological beliefs. And the fact that they are necessities does not get affected by the scholars' efforts in proving them as such in response to those who deny or doubt these truths, in the same way, their efforts in proving the specific Prophethood and physical resurrection – against the claims of those who follow the Qur'ān yet deny them as necessities of religion – do not undermine their axiomatic nature. In order to have a clearer understanding of the above, it would be supportive for you to read the following annex.

Annex

In the name of God ﷻ.

Religious necessities are divided into two parts:

1. A part considered necessary by all or most Muslims, such as the obligation of praying and fasting during the holy month of Ramadan.

2. A part considered amongst the necessities of a school of thought, such as the permissibility of combining the noon and evening prayers without necessity. Another example is the impurity of the dead animal even after undergoing a process of preservation. These things are considered amongst the necessities and axioms of the Shī'ī School of Thought, and whoever denies them while knowing that they are among the necessities of the Shī'ī School of Thought has stepped outside that school.

Whoever denies the necessities in the first part mentioned above has stepped outside of Islam.

This is regarding the necessary rulings; as for the beliefs that must be known by every dutiful person and adopted firmly, some of them are of the principles of faith such as Monotheism, specific Prophethood, and physical resurrection. And some of them are related to the principles of the Shīʿī School of Thought, such as believing in the Imāmate of the Imāms ﵈ after the Prophet ﷺ and believing in Divine Justice, which every dutiful person must adopt. Nonetheless, the absence of knowledge and belief in the former removes the person from the School of Islam, whereas its absence in the latter does not remove him from the school of Islam; it only removes him from the Shīʿī School of Thought of Ahl al-Bayt ﵈.

Believing in both parts, as mentioned by the scholars, is not a traditional matter; instead, the dutiful person must acquire this knowledge and adopt it as a belief, even though general evidence instills conviction. And the fact that these issues are considered among the principles of faith does not prevent well-informed and skilled scholars from studying them further and countering the arguments raised against them. Therefore, scholars specializing in ʿilm al-Kalām (the science of discourse) have researched Imāmate, as they did on the topics of specific Prophethood and the Hereafter.

And just like some schools discussed the issue of physical resurrection – and even the specific Prophethood; similarly, they discussed the issue of Imāmate. Nonetheless, these studies – whether in the principles of faith or school of thought – do not refute their necessary nature by those who prove them through conclusive evidence, even if some other schools do not approve of it. For, the efforts made by the scholars to prove these truths through evidence aim at refuting the suspicious claims raised by the other schools of thought, as they do not imply that these matters are subjected to Ijtihād for lack of clear designations or conclusive proof as evidence.

The necessities of the Shīʿī School of Thought (i.e., the matters of Imāmate and Divine Justice) are verified by conclusive evidence and clear to the extent that the scholars have prohibited the resort to Taqlīd in such matters. The path to acquiring this knowledge is accessible and facilitated for every dutiful person.

In conclusion, whether the beliefs are amongst the principles of faith or the school of thought is conclusive and necessary for all Muslims or believers. And any difference amongst the opinions of those who perform Ijtihād is related to the matters that are not considered among the necessities or axioms of the religion or school of thought, in which case it becomes necessary to verify these matters through evidence by resorting to the branches of faith. And since the ordinary person cannot verify the rulings, he must resort to Taqlīd.

Therefore, Ijtihād and Taqlīd are implemented in matters, not of the necessities and axioms. For, the necessities are only proved to refute the suspicious claims of the schools that do not believe in them as necessities – and this does not negate them being considered necessities by those who believe in them. And the issue of Imāmate, for the Shīʿa, is amongst these matters – as previously clarified. And God is the All-Knowing.

Miscellaneous Issues

Question 22:

What is your opinion in regards to those who comment on the Verse of the Guardians (Sūrat al-Nisā', Verse 95) as they make the following remark on the Imāmate Shī'ī scholars who say: "The intended meaning people therein are the twelve Infallible Imāms?"

The remark follows: "The order to obey someone does not necessarily imply his infallibility. The order may be mentioned in pursuit of emphasizing the credibility of his words - as in many other means of proof which God and the Prophet ordered us to adopt and use – during times in which we cannot verify something conclusively, like in many ḥadīths that guided towards resorting to scholars who may hit or miss in their understanding of the legal ruling. This is based on the observation of the balance between the positive consequences that rise upon following them and the negative consequences thereof. In light of the above, we cannot consider the command of obedience as proof for the infallibility of those referred to as the guardians without considering the ḥadīths mentioned in this regard."

Then, they said: "It is possible to consider the ḥadīths that stipulate that the intended people behind 'guardians' are the Infallible Imāms while adopting the wide interpretation of the term. This follows the approach adopted in the ḥadīths of Ahl al-Bayt which points out to the application under the title of interpretation to emphasize the futuristic movement of the Noble Qur'ān regarding the intellectual and practical matters that expand with the expansion of life itself."

Answer:

In the name of God ﷻ.

The command mentioned, in regards to following the jurists and scholars and adopting the ḥadīths narrated by trusted narrators, is but a guiding command that highlights the credibility and authenticity of their words as decided upon in the science of Uṣūl (the principles of jurisprudence). Therefore, it must be restricted - through the intellect - to the ignorance of its disagreement with reality. For, rendering something as a path to reality must have the likelihood of matching reality in the first place.

As for the command mentioned in the verse, it is a psychological and divine command. Whereby one cannot make this command absolute and inclusive of the idea that the Prophet may give the command ﷺ and the guardians in regards to an act that violated the command of God ﷻ, then it is rendered necessary – due to the absolute nature of the command to obey the Prophet ﷺ and the guardians – that the person who is absolutely and unrestrictedly obeyed is infallible. Thus, the intended people in verse are the Infallible Imāms عليهم السلام. This is also emphasized by linking the command to obey them with the command to obey God ﷻ and His Messenger ﷺ. And God is the One who guides us towards the straight path.

Divine Decree and Destiny

Question 23:

What is the opinion of the righteous sect regarding those who restrict the divine decree and destiny to the creational reality rather than the social one? For, they respond to Shaykh Muḥammad b.

Muḥammad b. Nuʿmān Mufīd says: "The issues of Divine Decree and Destiny do not have any connection to the commands and prohibitions issued by God regarding the obligations related to His servants' actions. They are rather connected to the creational and human realities, in terms of that which God created and established, and the nature of these creations to the extent with which man can have a detailed and clear impression of the reasons dwelling behind it all – that is, creation, its causes and its purpose."

They clarified further in another context: "There is no such thing called Divine Decree and Destiny. Man is the one who creates his decree and destiny. Nonetheless, there is historical determinism; and there are political and economic determinisms. When you talk to a person about his deterministic events, you isolate him from all that surrounds him. However, when God speaks of Divine Decree and Destiny, He says to you: You create your decree and destiny... until He says: We do not say that the current state of things represents divine decree and destiny; for, the current reality is that which has been created by others and impacted by certain objective circumstances!"

Answer:

In the name of God ﷻ.

Divine Decree and Destiny are divided into two parts:

1. That is related to the servant's choice, such as winning and losing. For, man's will impacts this. And God's ﷻ knowledge of its occurrence due to the servant's choice is not a reason that led the servant to engage in that work.

2. That which is not related to the servant's will. This is the inevitable decree, such as wealth, poverty, lifespans, and other matters that are out of the servant's hands. This is manifested in the Noble Qur'ān such as in His ﷻ saying:

﴿قُل لَّن يُصِيبَنَا إِلَّا مَا كَتَبَ اللَّهُ﴾

﴿*qul lan yuṣībanā ʾillā mā kataba llāhu*﴾

﴿Say, *'Nothing will befall us except what God has ordained for us*﴾[32]

---

[32] Sūrat al-Tawbah, Verse 51.

and His ﷻ saying:

﴿إِنَّا أَنزَلْنَاهُ فِي لَيْلَةِ الْقَدْرِ﴾

﴾ʾinnā ʾanzalnāhu fī laylati l-qadrⁱ﴿

﴾Indeed We sent it down on the Night of Ordainment﴿*[33]

Per the narrations, the meaning behind the night of destiny is the night of decreeing sustenance, lifespans, and its likes. And God is the One who guides towards righteousness.

Moral and Religious Values

Question 24:

What is the opinion of the Sacred Legislator, on the overall level, in regards to those who say the following: "The divine values are not absolute; rather, there are boundaries to these values that stem from the realistic life of man in regards to his natural needs on Earth." And after they speak

---

[33] Sūrat al-Qadr, Verse 1.

* That is, the Qur'ān. See 44:2-5.

about the legislative exceptions – such as the case with the permissibility of lying in certain situations and the impermissibility of being honest therein – they say: "Based on these premises, the moral value – even in religions – is relative." That is why the fundamentalists say: "There is no general principle except that it has a certain specificity?"

Answer:

In the name of God ﷻ.

The restriction of legal rulings, such as the prohibition of lying, to the absence of harm has no connection to the fundamentalists' saying, "There is no general principle except that it has a certain specificity." For, in this saying, the fundamentalists are addressing the world of al-Ithbāt[34] and not that of al-Thubūt[35]. The legal ruling in matters of thubūt is either absolute, from the beginning, or narrow and limited. Thus, specificity and

[34] Translator's Note: An uṣūl term related to what is apparent and subjected to means of proof.

[35] Translator's Note: An uṣūl term related to the actual reality of things.

exceptions are not reasonably plausible in matters of thubūt

As for the religious and moral values, some are relative – such as the hideousness of lying and beauty of honesty – and others are absolute – such as the ugliness of oppression and beauty of justice. God is the One Who guides towards righteousness.

The Straight Path and the Scale

Question 25:

What is the opinion of the noble legislator in regards to those who consider The Straight Path to be mere symbolistic, whereby they say: "The word does not express something materialistic; for, the Noble Qur'ān did not mention the straight path except in the context of the way or course which expresses the path taken by man towards his good or evil purposes in life. Therefore, talking about accuracy while envisioning The Straight Path in the Hereafter is a symbol for the precision of distinguishing the path of integrity from the path of deviation... knowing that there are plenty of ḥadīths on behalf of the Infallibles عليهم السلام in regards to the embodiment and material representation of The Straight Path?

Answer:

In the name of God ﷻ.

It is mandatory for a Muslim to believe in The Straight Path, the scale, and other matters of the Hereafter, as they are in reality, and to regard them as indubitable truths. As for the claim that The Straight Path is symbolic needs to have the proper knowledge; even the exoteric meaning of religious designations points to the actual existence of the straight path.

And God is All-Knowing.

The Well-Informed Man and Legal Rulings

Question 26:

Does the well-informed man have the right to determine Islamic thoughts and concepts and be opinionated in Islamic matters (besides legal rulings)? And do we have the right to consider his views or opinions? Or, due to his lack of seminary students, must we refer to scholars in these matters?

Answer:

In the name of God ﷻ.

One must refer to scholars; this is the intended meaning behind God's words:

﴿فاسألوا أهلَ الذِّكرِ إن كُنتُم لا تَعلَمونَ﴾

﴿*fa-s'alū 'ahla dh-dhikri 'in kuntum lā ta'lamūna*﴾

﴿*ask the People of the Reminder if you do not know*﴾[36]

And God is the All-Knowing.

---

[36] Sūrat al-Naḥl, Verse 43.

The Book and the Stamp

Question 27:

It is mentioned[37] that the Imāms عليهم السلام pass upon one another a stamped book as a legacy or stamps (Vol. 1, book of, chapter which mentions that the Imāms have not done anything and do not do anything save upon the delegation of God) which each of them open and sign what is in it. It is also mentioned that Imām al-Ḥusayn عليه السلام opened it and found in it (the message): "If the killer is found, then kill and be killed, and bring out the people for bearing witness." Emerge with people towards martyrdom, and you will not realize martyrdom except with them." So, he did. It is also stated that Imām Zayn al-ʿĀbidīn عليه السلام opened it and saw the following: "Remain silent and quiet." And Imām Muḥammad al-Bāqir عليه السلام opened the fifth stamp and found in it the following: "Interpret the book of God, believe and make others believe your father, pass the inheritance to your son and create the nation...and so on."

---

[37] Kulaynī, Shaykh Muḥammad b. Yaʿqūb, *al-Kāfī*, Vol. 1, in the book of *al-Ḥujjah* in the chapter mentioning that the Imāms have not done anything and do not do anything save upon the delegation of God.

What is your opinion in regards to what some Islamic writers and intellectuals do in terms of analyzing the history of the Imāms ﷺ and deducing opinions and stances from their records, and then presenting this analysis in their writings in a way in which the reader understands it as an explanation of the event and a justification for the Infallibles' ﷺ actions? Do they have the right to do that? How is this related to the narrations that mention the book and the stamps?

Answer:

In the name of God ﷻ.

It is well-established that some Imāms ﷺ had unique circumstances and positions that differ from others. A good example is the age of Imām Alī b. Abī Ṭālib ﷺ;, the significant events during that period need honest reflection and deep research to fully understand. Many people who analyzed the events fell into great confusion; for it was difficult for some to understand the silence of Imām Alī b. Abī Ṭālib ﷺ in response to what happened to the caliphate and other events.

Moreover, the circumstances of Imām al-Ḥasan ‎ and the oppression that befell him are different from the age of Imām al-Ḥusayn. For, Imām al-Ḥasan was surrounded by difficult circumstances which forced him to sign a treaty with Muʿāwīya b. Abī Sufyān, upon which he was abandoned by those who were close and distant from him. Perhaps, whoever is well-informed about the Imāms conditions and what they were exposed to during their times will benefit from their speeches and actions. Some of their actions were not restricted to certain times; therefore, one can adopt the action performed by the Imām in the circumstances that match those times and add some religious speeches, such as those that tackled the treatment of innovators, oppressors, and others. Thus, one can deduct, from the totality of these incidents, a legal ruling specific to him or general to all believers or a specific group thereof.

In other words, the historical accounts of the Imāms and their actions constitute legal proof of the obligation to do a specific act or its permissibility based on the deduction of those well-informed about their conditions. God does not order them to do anything unless it contributes to their betterment and the greater good of Islam. This is their عليهم السلام proof for the upcoming generations so that people can know that circumstances vary. For, some circumstances may require silence, while, in other circumstances, the greater good may require the rising against the oppressor – with different levels of rising – like in the case of Imām al-Ḥusayn عليه السلام after the mandate of Muʿāwīya b. Abī Sufyān had ended. People saw what Muʿāwīya b. Abī Sufyān did this after gaining power and control over them and playing with the religion of God عز وجل. For this sake, Imām al-Ḥusayn عليه السلام rose; and he knew that it was an order issued by God عز وجل and well-received from His Messenger ﷺ. And his actions عليه السلام were proof, so people realized that the one sitting on the caliph's throne was not qualified to reign. Instead, the caliphate belongs to those who are deserving and competent. In conclusion, there is no reservation against the analysis of the history of Ahl al-Bayt عليهم السلام and the manifestation of their approaches and ways of interaction with different circumstances. However, these actions must be carried out by the elite scholars and jurists who are well-informed, have deep knowledge of the Noble Qur'ān and the ḥadīths of Ahl al-Bayt عليهم السلام and are skilled in understanding the Imam's عليهم السلام

thoughts and intentions behind their speeches and actions. And God is All-Knowing.

The Source of Theological Principles

Question 28:

A saying goes: "Theological beliefs are rational matters that must be reached by the dutiful person directly after he knows its proof and surrenders to it. He must not adopt these beliefs through Taqlīd."

Does this include all theological beliefs, or only its principles and foundations, excluding the details? What about the details that are debated? What is the reference that determines what is correct and more truthful? Are theological beliefs subjected to the rules and sciences through which legal rulings are studied, such that we can refer them to a specialized expert, or can we, as ordinary people, deal with them directly?

For example, in regards to the narrations that speak of the limits of the Imam's عليه السلام knowledge (for instance), can we refute it since rational necessity does not consider it a requirement for the Imām and since it only imposes upon him the infallibility in making mistakes related to spreading the message – exclusively – or, should we surrender, yield and believe in them (in case it is considered valid in terms of authenticity and proof)?

Answer:

In the name of God ﷻ.

The principles of theological belief are divided into two parts:

1. That one must build upon, believe wholeheartedly, and yield to the events and conditions that follow death, including the matters of the grave, the judgment, the book, the straight path, the scale, Heaven, hell, and others. It is not incumbent on the dutiful person to acquire the knowledge related to the details of the matters above; he must believe wholeheartedly and build upon the reality which was disseminated by the Prophet ﷺ or the Guardian ؏.

2. That which must be known through intellect or religion, such as the knowledge of God ﷻ and His prophets ؏ and friends, who are the

Infallible Imāms ع, in addition to their legal rulings and interpretation and exegesis of the Noble Qur'ān. As for the rest of the specificities, it is enough to believe in them; and it is not permissible to deny or refute what has been mentioned regarding their ع knowledge and other affairs, even if one does not find an authentic narration that proves it – let alone in case he finds a correct narration that proves it. In conclusion, the one who commits intellectual disobedience must turn – in every discipline or knowledge – to the experts in that knowledge. In regards to the science of theological belief, one must turn to the scholars and jurists who have studied the science of discourse deeply, understood the Noble Qur'ān and the ḥadīths of Ahl al-Bayt ع, and have gained the skill of distinguishing right from wrong – especially the Marji's of each school of thought and its scholars. And God is All-Knowing.

Jurists are the Custodians over Theological Beliefs

Question 29:

Regarding the just jurists who meet all the conditions for legal rulings and Taqlīd and who are the custodians over the jurisprudence of the Prophet's Household ﷺ, are they custodians over theological beliefs as well? Is it permissible for some to say that they – God forbids – support and adopt myths and legends to be considerate towards the general public due to their fear of them or their devotion to maintaining a connection with them?

Answer:

In the name of God ﷻ.

The role of the scholars is to clarify the permissible and impermissible acts, in addition to manifesting the moral theological beliefs and the corruption that results from false theological beliefs, which some people mistake for true religion. And what is said regarding their negligence towards false beliefs out of fear of losing connection with people is baseless and utterly false. Yes, they do not strike something that does not transgress against religion and maintains the possibility of being correct. Moreover, in certain situations, they observe what is important and what is more important. They also gradually manifest false or corrupt beliefs amongst people, such as when people have newly adopted the path of religiosity. This took place during the early stages of Islam and during the times of the Imāms ﷺ. And God is All-Knowing.

A Paragraph from the Supplication of Rajab

Question 30:

It is kindly requested that you clarify the meaning of the following expressions which were mentioned in the Supplication of Rajab: "...I ask You for what You spoke through them of Your will, so You made them reserves for Your words, and pillars of Your monotheism, verses and stations that are not suspended in every place that knows You. There is no difference between You and them, except that they are Your servants and creation."

Answer:

The pronoun "them" in the phrase "there is no difference between You and them" refers to "Your verse," which is represented by the Imāms عليهم السلام. It has, therefore, become clear that the pronoun in "except they are Your servants" also refers to the Imāms عليهم السلام. As for his saying, "I ask You for what You spoke through them of Your will", it refers to God's ﷻ word, which was expressed in the Noble Qur'ān through His saying:

﴿إِنَّمَا أَمْرُهُ إِذَا أَرَادَ شَيْئًا أَن يَقُولَ لَهُ كُن فَيَكُونُ﴾

﴿*'innamā 'amruhū 'idhā 'arāda shay'an 'an yaqūla lahū kun fa-yakūnu*﴾

﴿*All His command, when He wills something, is to say to it 'Be,' and it is*﴾[38]

This has also been implied in the Verse of Purification, which indicates that what distinguishes the pure Imāms عليهم السلام from other people is not acquired; instead, it is related to God's will ﷻ – as shown in the Verse of Purification as well. Yes, God's ﷻ will indeed is preceded by His

[38] Sūrat Yasīn, Verse 82.

knowledge of their distinct obedience to God ﷻ – which would not have changed if He ﷻ did not grant them all that His ﷻ will determine, as mentioned in the Supplication of al-Nudba. And God is All-Knowing.

Knowing the Positions of the Imāms عليهم السلام

Question 31:

Some people see the position of the Imāms عليهم السلام, their stations, miracles, and precedence over the rest of mankind. This is not important; it is mere intellectual indulgence. Applying their teachings and abiding by their عليهم السلام guidance must be genuinely cared for. Observing the first aspect distracts and impacts the second aspect negatively. What is your opinion on the matter?

Answer:

In the name of God ﷻ.

It is required that every believer knows his Imām عليه السلام as much as he can and the fact that he is assigned by God ﷻ through the will of the Messenger of God ﷺ per what God ordered him ﷻ.

Moreover, he must know that the Imāms ﷺ are infallible and that reflecting on the positions of Ahl al-Bayt ﷺ, their intellectual and practical statuses, and their unseen characteristics is plausible; for it supports the believer in increasing his faith in the Imāms ﷺ, holding him steadfast upon their path and keeping him persistent in defending them and their school of thought. And this is considered to be one of the greatest means of proximity and grandest Islamic work, unlike the person who is not interested in knowing the virtues of Ahl al-Bayt ﷺ and their positions; whereby he does not find within himself any enthusiasm to defend the Shīʿī School of Thought and to serve and embed the true theological beliefs. And God is All-Knowing.

The Prophets and Imāms ﷺ are Exceptions from the Undesirable Acts of Burial

Question 32:

It is mentioned in the chapter on the "undesirable actions during the burial", of the book al-ʿUrwa al-Wuthqa, that: (...Seventh: renewing the grave after it fades except for the graves of the prophets, guardians, virtuous people, and scholars... Ninth: building upon it except for the graves mentioned; it also seems that burying a grave under a building or a ceiling is not undesirable... Tenth: Using the cemetery as a mosque except for the graves of prophets, Imāms, and scholars... Eleventh: building shrines on graves except the prophets' and Imāms'...) What is the reason behind excluding these graves from the aforementioned undesirable acts? And what is your opinion regarding the adornments and decorations in these shrines?

Answer:

In the name of God ﷻ.

The reason is that the Prophets عليهم السلام and Imāms عليهم السلام graves are monuments of guidance and a haven for the people on this Earth. The same applies to their pure descendants, companions, and scholars who narrate their ḥadīths and follow them. Establishing shrines on their عليهم السلام graves is honoring the sacraments

﴿ذَٰلِكَ وَمَن يُعَظِّمْ شَعَائِرَ اللَّهِ فَإِنَّهَا مِن تَقْوَى الْقُلُوبِ﴾

﴿dhālika wa-man yuʿaẓẓim shaʿāʾira llāhi fa-ʾinnahā min taqwā l-qulūb[1]*﴾*

﴾*That. And whoever venerates the sacraments of God —indeed that arises from the Godwariness of hearts*﴿[39]

And the prohibition above of ornaments is implemented in mosques. And God is All-Knowing.

Rāq and Beseeching the Imāms عليهم السلام for Getting Cured

Question 33:

What is the explanation of the verse:

﴿كَلَّا إِذا بَلَغَتِ التَّراقِيَ﴾

﴾*kallā ʾidhā balaghati t-tarāqiya*﴿

﴿وَقيلَ مَنْ ۜ راقٍ﴾

﴾*wa-qīla man rāqin*﴿

[39] Sūrat al-Ḥajj, Verse 32.

﴾No indeed! When the soul reaches up to the collar bones, and it is said, 'Who will take him up?'﴿[40]

What is the meaning of "Rāq"? Do you offer corrections to what was mentioned in certain narrations, such as lamenting when reading certain supplications, adopting amulets to seek safety, getting cured of a disease, and so on? How can one balance between these actions and the necessity of consulting a doctor and resorting to the natural and physical causes of recovery?

Answer:

In the name of God ﷻ.

And it said: "Who will take him up." This is the saying of man when he experiences death, upon which he forgets everything except himself. So, he asks – even wishes – for someone to cure him. He then becomes confident of separating from the

---

[40] Sūrat al-Qiyāmah, Verse 26-27.

* That is, by the angels of mercy and the angels of wrath present at the side of the dying person, as to which of them will take charge of him. Or those who are present by the side of the dying person say, 'Where is the medicine man?'

world and his loved ones. Thus, his fluctuation does not mean that God will not heal him from what has befallen him if God's will to cure him is connected to his beseechment, his parents, loved ones, or virtuous people's beseechment of the prophets and Imāms ﷺ and so on.

It goes without saying that what is mentioned in some supplications is required by the legislator, yet, it does not necessarily have the intended impact, even if God ﷻ knows it is not good for the person. As for getting cured by resorting to other supplications is similar to the cure mentioned in the Noble Qur'ān, in Sūrat al-Naml:

﴿فِيهِ شِفَاءٌ لِلنَّاسِ﴾

﴿*fīhi shifā'un li-n-nāsi*﴾

﴿*in which there is a cure for the people*﴾[41]

Therefore, supplicating to God ﷻ and turning to the doctor, knowing that God's will to cure him is connected to his action, is plausible. For, if he supplicated or has someone who supplicated for

[41] Sūrat al-Naḥl, Verse 69.

him or resorted to the doctor or beseeched the Imāms ﷺ, then God ﷻ will cure him if He ﷻ wills.

And God is All-Knowing.

Contradictory Sayings

Question 34:

Suppose all these sayings come from one person, despite originating from various schools of thought. Can we rely on what this person raises regarding theological beliefs or jurisprudential opinions? And what is the appropriate way to deal with those who consider such behavior an intentional attempt to instill doubt about the infallibility of the Imāms ﷺ in the followers of the Shīʿī School of Thought? They claim that had he used one opinion; we could have said that his words represent him solely. However, his words sprung from different – and contradictory – schools of thought. Then they shared their thoughts in front of the public, knowing he spoke about these issues in gatherings, general assemblies, radio, and TV. He published his words in books, newspapers, magazines, and social media accounts.

Answer:

In the name of God ﷻ.

The answer to this question has been manifested in previous ones. And God is the One who guides us towards the straight path.

The Love of Ahl al-Bayt ﷺ

Question 35:

Does the mere love of Ahl al-Bayt ﷺ and hatred of their enemies benefit a person if it does not push him towards worship and action?

Answer:

In the name of God ﷻ.

The love of Ahl al-Bayt ﷺ, following them, and seeking their proximity are all obligations incumbent on every person based on the Qur'ānic designations and Sunnah. And whoever contains hatred towards them is considered outside Islam. Ahl al-Bayt ﷺ ordered us not to rely on their love in a way that makes us heedless of taking action. Therefore, what is falsely claimed about the Shīʿa in regards to them entirely relying on their belief in the guardianship of the Imāms (|D) and refraining from taking any action is a false accusation. As for the penalty for those who love them yet do not perform good deeds or commit misdeeds, it is to be determined by God ﷻ. Hopefully, good things will befall them because of the good that they did – that is, loving and following them. Moreover, God's ﷻ mercy and the intercession of His Prophet ﷺ and his Pure Household ﷷ may embrace him. And perhaps the narrated ḥadīth, "The love of Ali is a good deed with which no misdeed can cause harm," refers to this origin; yet, it does not imply the absolute promise or oath of receiving intercession.

The Return (Rajʿa)

Question 36:

What do you say regarding the Return (Rajʿa)? Is it correct to consider it one of the principles of the Shīʿī School of Thought?

Answer:

It is not of the principles of the Shīʿī School of Thought. However, it is proved with conclusive certainty due to authentic narrations, which can generally be considered amongst the frequently narrated ḥadīths. And God is All-Knowing.

The Bodies and Souls of the Imāms عليهم السلام

Question 37:

In regards to the ḥadīth that mentions the formation of the drop of fluid from which Sayyidah Fāṭimah al-Zahrāʾ عليها السلام was created, the food that used to be offered to the Prophet صلى الله عليه وآله and his isolation from Sayyidah Khadījah عليها السلام, is it related to the creation of her عليها السلام soul or blessed body? And generally, does the form and body of the infallible person differ from that of the rest of humanity? How did they get sick, then? How come some of them had a very dark skin color and some were fat, as per the narrations? How accurate are the claims that suggest that the Infallibles عليهم السلام had unique bodily characteristics, such as the claim that they did not sleep and that they saw all the people as if they were right in front of them, and that their footprints would be traced on rocks even without the presence of sand?

Answer:

In the name of God ﷻ.

In regards to the characteristics of their souls and bodies, we mentioned in a previous response that God's ﷻ will be attached to granting them unique characteristics in their bodies and souls that is unmatched by anyone else.

As for the characteristic being in the absence of sleep or the ability to see all creation or otherwise, as mentioned in some narrations, it is better to refer this matter to the experts.

Moreover, the Infallibles' عليهم السلام capacity to know whatever they want to know is well-established. For, if they desired to know something, they would know it. As for the inquiry of how they managed to acquire that knowledge and whether it took place by having the infallible person directed towards the unknown and then acquiring that knowledge or through the Sacred Spirit which accompanies them, or by conversing with the angels or by inspiration, we do not have an obligation to know its details and means. And God is All-Knowing.

The Knowledge of Deaths and Calamities

Question 38:

If Amīr al-Mu'minīn ﷺ gave some of his companions, such as Rashīd al-Ḥijrī and Salmān al-Fārisī, the knowledge of deaths and calamities, then he ﷺ – himself – had this knowledge as well. Thus, he knew his lifespan and the time of his death. In light of the above, what is the case in regards to Amīr al-Mu'minīn ﷺ sleeping in the Prophet's ﷺ mattress on the Night of Emigration (Hijra), and what is the case with his confrontation of 'Amr b. 'Abdiwudd on the day of al-Khandaq – amongst other dangerous and life-threatening situations he encountered?

Answer:

In the name of God ﷻ.

Amīr al-Mu'minīn ﷺ used to know that which lies in the tablet of erasure and establishment; this knowledge does not negate the reality that he acted without knowing its condition in the tablet of destiny. That is why performing a certain deed in response to God ﷻ or His Messenger's order ﷺ – be it general or specific – does not negate the impact of obedience without knowledge of that action within the tablet of destiny. Accordingly, the Imam's ؑ knowledge of the date of his death can be considered al-Badā' (change in Divine Will and Decree) due to its mismatch of the tablet of destiny. Secondly, God ﷻ may conceal from His ﷻ infallible friend, mainly the date of his death.

The History of Ḥusaynī Sacraments

Question 39:

What is your opinion on the Ḥusaynī sacraments? And what do you say to those who claim that they are newly-established rituals which did not exist in the times of the pure Imāms ؑ and, therefore, are illegitimate?

Answer:

In the name of God ﷻ.

The Shīʿa, during the times of the Imāms عليهم السلام, used to live in a state of Taqiyyah (concealing one's true faith or beliefs in protecting their wellbeing and their loved ones); and they used to establish mourning appearances according to what was possible for them. And the absence of sacraments in their time was, like our time, due to its infeasibility. This does not imply its illegitimacy in our time. Had it been possible for the Shīʿa to express and establish those sacraments, they would have – just like we did in raising black flags on doors of Ḥusseiniyyat as an expression of sadness. And whoever reads the history of the Ziyarah (visitation) of Imām al-Ḥusayn عليه السلام during the time of the Infallibles عليهم السلام will realize this truth. If that were an innovation, it would also be an innovation since it did not take place during the Infallibles عليهم السلام.

Thus, all these sacraments fall under the sacraments of God عزّ وجلّ and are meant to express sadness over the calamities which befell Imām al-Ḥusayn عليه السلام, his family, his companions and the rest of the Imāms عليهم السلام, which have all been proven to be legitimate and also desirable; for, it is considered amongst the greatest means through which one can seek proximity to God عزّ وجلّ. God عزّ وجلّ says:

﴿ذَٰلِكَ وَمَن يُعَظِّمْ شَعَائِرَ اللَّهِ فَإِنَّهَا مِن تَقْوَى الْقُلُوبِ﴾

﴿dhālika wa-man yuʿaẓẓim shaʿāʾira llāhi fa-ʾinnahā min taqwā l-qulūbⁱ﴾

﴿That. And whoever venerates the sacraments of God —indeed that arises from the Godwariness of hearts﴾[42]

Imām Muḥammad al-Bāqir ﷺ said to al-Fudayl b. Yasar: "Do you sit and talk?" I said: "yes", he said: "I love these gatherings. So, revive our stories; for, whoever sits in a gathering where our stories are revived, his heart will not die on the day when hearts die." And God is the All-Knowing.

Taqiyyah

Question 40:

Kindly comment on the following paragraph mentioned by Āyatullāh al-Khūʾī in his study of the divisions of Taqiyyah, amongst which is the prohibited Taqiyyah: "If the corruption ensued upon the act of Taqiyyah is greater than that ensued upon forsaking that act, or if the benefit of

---

[42] Sūrat al-Ḥajj, Verse 32.

forsaking Taqiyyah is greater than that ensued upon adopting it - such as if one knows that if he acts with Taqiyyah righteousness will shrink, the original religion will fade, falsehood will rise, and oppression will be promoted, and if he forsakes Taqiyyah then he will only get killed, or he will get killed with other groups – then, it is undebatable that the obligation is to forsake Taqiyyah and train the spirit to be killed; for, the corruption that ensues upon Taqiyyah is greater and more severe than the corrupt action of getting killed."

Then he says: "Perhaps, this is why Imām al-Ḥusayn ﵇ and his companions went forward in fighting Yazīd b. Muʿāwīya b. Abī Sufyān exposed themselves to the risk of martyrdom and forsook the adoption of Taqiyyah with Yazīd. Likewise, this was followed by some of the companions of Amīr al-Mu'minīn ﵇ and by some of our virtuous scholars (May God bless their souls and reward them the best of rewards) such as the two martyrs and others."[43]

Answer:

In the name of God ﷻ.

[43] *Al-Tanqīḥ*, Vol. 4, p. 257.

The prohibited Taqiyyah is that if one acts upon it, he protects himself from harm; however, his actions result in general and more critical harm, such as the harm inflicted on the landmarks of religion and causing corruption within the society or maintaining it. For, the person would then know that the legislator disapproves of the presence of that corruption or its continuity. Thus, in this case, it is prohibited to act upon Taqiyyah.

The mandatory Taqiyyah is the exact opposite, for observing this type of Taqiyyah eliminates a certain type of corruption. And forsaking it and carrying out the original action only fulfills unnecessary interests.

As for the cause of Imām al-Ḥusayn ﷷ, the interest (of Islam) lay in his martyrdom at the hands of the oppressive enemies who usurped the caliphate rather than acting upon Taqiyyah. Imām al-Ḥusayn ﷷ fulfilled his objectives whereby his martyrdom resulted in the ruin of their caliphate; such that had he not risen, this significant effect included the preservation of the Islamic religion and the school of the pure and infallible Ahl al-Bayt عليهم السلام would not have ensued.

The rise of Imām al-Ḥusayn ﷷ was a wake-up call for people from their deep sleep and heedlessness. It manifested the true theological beliefs that must be followed and preserved so that the upcoming generations could benefit from his uprising ﷷ. And God is the All-Knowing.

The Knowledge of the Imāms ﷷ

Question 41:

It is attributed to your Eminence that you believe that the knowledge of the Prophet ﷺ and the guiding Imāms ﷷ is present knowledge rather than acquired knowledge and that they are aware of all that God ﷻ knows. You also mentioned that their ﷷ knowledge is of presence and comprehensiveness rather than acquisition and informing. They create, provide sustenance, bring to life, and take life away. Miracles are not divine acts manifested at their hands; instead, God ﷻ rendered them the actors of all mentioned above. Are these words true? How true is that which was attributed to your Eminence?

Answer:

In the name of God ﷻ.

This attribution is incorrect. We, generally, think that they are knowledgeable in all which God ﷻ has taught them out of his bountifulness and kindness and in response to what they and the people need. They generally have creational guardianship and are actors, with God's ﷻ creational permission, of what is beneficial according to them. And God ﷻ is the Creator, Sustainer, the One who brings life, and the One who takes life away. And peace be upon you.

The Imāms عليهم السلام are the Intermediaries of Divine Emanation

Question 42:

Is it permissible to believe that the Prophet ﷺ and the Infallible Imāms عليهم السلام are the active, physical, and virtual cause, in addition to being the purpose for all creation?

Is it permissible to describe them using such terms? What is the ruling regarding those who believe in the above?

Answer:

In the name of God ﷻ.

First: They are the intermediaries of divine emanation for those who beseech them; for God ﷻ says:

﴿وَابتَغوا إِلَيهِ الوَسيلَةَ﴾

﴾wa-btaghū ʾilayhi l-wasīlata﴿

﴾And seek the means of recourse to Him﴿[44]

They are the purpose in the sense that they have attained the highest levels of worship, which is the purpose of all creation, as per God's ﷻ saying:

﴿وَما خَلَقتُ الجِنَّ وَالإِنسَ إِلّا لِيَعبُدونِ﴾

﴾wa-mā khalaqtu l-jinna wa-l-ʾinsa ʾillā li-ya ʿbudūni﴿

[44] Sūrat al-Māʾidah, Verse 35.

⟪I did not create the jinn and the humans except that they may worship Me⟫[45]

Second: Using these terms is not right. The proper terms to use are the ones we have mentioned.

Third: If the intention of those who use these terms when describing them ☙ is to say that this power is granted to them ☙ by God ☙, and if he understands and interprets these terms in a way that does not negate God's ☙ deity, then he is not said to have stepped out of the Shīʿī School of Thought. Otherwise, he would be considered among the exaggerators. And God is All-Knowing.

The Physical Creation of the Imāms

Question 43:

What is your opinion in regards to those who believe that the Prophet ☙ and his Holy Household ☙ were present with their souls and physical bodies before the creation of this world and that they were created before Ādam ☙ – rather than having God ☙ create their virtual images around the Throne?

---

[45] Sūrat al-Dhāriyāt, Verse 56.

Answer:

In the name of God ﷻ.

They ﷺ were present with their luminous shadows before creating Ādam ؑ. And their physical creation took place after the creation of Ādam ؑ, as clearly demonstrated.

And God is the All-Knowing.

Annex

To His Eminence, a set of questions was raised by a group of students from the University of Kuwait.

Your Eminence, the Grand Āyatullāh, Āyatullāh Mīrzā Jawād Tabrīzī,

May God's peace and blessings be upon you.

We are a group of students at the University of Kuwait, eager to acquire Islamic knowledge, religious sciences, theological beliefs, and the conditions of our Imāms عليهم السلام. We ask you, Your Eminence, for permission to receive from the bountifulness of your answers to some of our theological questions and matters related to guardianship. We do not have anyone after our Master – the Master of our Time عجل الله تعالى فرجه الشريف, save you who defend Islam, preserve the rulings and provisions, and guide the people. Therefore, O' Master, O' representative of the infallible Imam عجل الله تعالى فرجه الشريف, do not deprive us of the sparks of your knowledge or cast us away from the door of your sciences. And guide us towards righteousness and the rewarding place. May God عز وجل protect you and preserve you as a treasure for the Muslims. May God عز وجل make you successful until the Day of Judgment.

First Question

Do the narrations that speak of the presence of Amīr al-Mu'minīn عليه السلام in the grave and on the deathbed point out to actual presence? And if so, how does this balance out the idea that the limited entity cannot be present in multiple places at once? Or, are these narrations guided and interpreted; for some claim that they imply that the follower will see the fruit of following Amīr al-Mu'minīn عليه السلام and the master of the guardians عليه السلام?

Answer:

In the name of God عز وجل: He appears with his luminous existence, not in his physical existence. The former was created before the latter, as mentioned in authentic narrations. And his luminous existence does not negate any of the raised reservations, such as the multiplicity of his existence in several places simultaneously. And God is All-Knowing.

Second Question

Is believing in the creational delegation to the Imāms عليهم السلام permissible? And if so, would creational guardianship be considered a power entrusted to the infallible person, or does he (the infallible person) ask God ﷻ and receive from there?

Answer:

In the name of God ﷻ: Believing in the delegation is null and void. For God ﷻ carries through His ﷻ commands, and the Imāms ﷺ are intermediaries and intercessors between them and God ﷻ in regards to supplicating and asking God ﷻ for needs. God ﷻ says:

﴿وَابتَغوا إِلَيهِ الوَسيلَةَ﴾

﴿*wa-btaghū 'ilayhi l-wasīlata*﴾

﴿*And seek the means of recourse to Him*﴾[46]

And we do not know a means greater than the Prophet ﷺ and the Imāms ﷺ, who have creational guardianship. This was also established for other Prophets ﷺ, which are better than the other Prophets ﷺ. And divine wisdom requires that, perhaps, they are acting in a creational manner to avert the harm of those who intend harm to the

[46] Sūrat al-Mā'idah, Verse 35.

religion and Muslims. The Imāms عليهم السلام has a distinction over the rest of the Prophets عليهم السلام; for the Prophets عليهم السلام proved their Prophethood through miracles and breaching norms, unlike the Imāms عليهم السلام whose Imāmate was established by the assignment of the Messenger of God ﷺ. And they are the keys with which people are tried after the Prophet ﷺ, as mentioned in the Al-Zīyārah al-Jāmiʿa. That is why their creational actions were only a few; they did not act upon people's suggestions. Instead, they acted as such in rare situations whenever wisdom and necessity demanded it, especially when they nullified and invalidated some claims of Prophethood or Imāmate. And God is All-Knowing.

Third Question

Is it permissible for the Shīʿa follower to say that the infallible Imām عليه السلام granted him this specific form of sustenance or that he knew the unforeseen without saying "with God's permission", knowing that whoever says this usually believes that all of this is done upon delegation by God ﷻ?

Answer:

In the name of God ﷻ: If he does not believe that God ﷻ is the One ﷻ who provides him with sustenance and that the Imām ﷺ is an intermediary for requesting abundant or appropriate sustenance from God ﷻ – whereby he believed that the Imām ﷺ is the one ﷺ who provides sustenance rather than an intermediary in the emanation – then his belief is null and void. For he then enters into false delegation. As for their knowledge of the Unseen, they know only as much as God ﷻ has taught them. For God ﷻ is the All-Knowing of the Unseen, and He ﷻ does not share this knowledge with anyone except an apostle He ﷻ approves of. Then He ﷻ dispatches a sentinel before and behind him. And God is the All-Knowing.

Fourth Question

Is it permissible to mention the virtues of the Infallibles ﷺ and share them in gatherings and ceremonies without verifying the authenticity of these narrations' chain of transmission?

Answer:

In the Name of God ﷻ: If the importance of the narration is not established, then it can be done as a sort of storytelling from a certain book, as long as its falsehood has not been known. And God is the All-Knowing.

Fifth Question

Is it permissible to say that God ﷻ delegated some of His ﷻ affairs to the Imāms ﷺ? And if so, what is the difference between false and true delegations?

Answer:

In the name of God ﷻ: We have mentioned already that the school of thought which endorses delegation is false. For, God ﷻ says:

﴿وَابتَغوا إِلَيهِ الوَسيلَةَ﴾

﴾*wa-btaghū 'ilayhi l-wasīlata*﴿

﴾*And seek the means of recourse to Him*﴿[47]

---

[47] Sūrat al-Mā'idah, Verse 35.

And God is the All-Knowing.

Sixth Question

Is Ḥadīth al-Kisāʾ verified utilizing an authentic chain or narrations? What is the reward for those who read this honorable ḥadīth?

Answer:

In the name of God ﷻ: Ḥadīth al-Kisāʾ is quite famous, and the reward that has been mentioned is granted to the reader, to whoever beseeches this ḥadīth and to those who were addressed in this ḥadīth ﷺ during times of need. And God is All-Knowing.

Seventh Question

There are some gatherings conducted by women called "the completion of Sūrat al-Anʿām", where this Sūrah is read in a specific way whereby the reader pauses when he comes across certain verses in order to read some supplications and repeats them several times. My question to you, O' Master, is the following: Are not such gatherings considered amongst the innovations since they were not mentioned in any religious designation nor proved nor conducted during the days of the Messenger of God ﷺ or the pure Imāms ؑ? We also request, from your Eminence, to provide us with a definition for the prohibited innovation.

Answer:

In the name of God ﷻ: Innovation claims that something not part of religion is part of it regarding rulings and provisions, laws, and making illegitimate worship legitimate according to religion. This does not apply to reading a Sūrah or supplication in a specific manner if it is with the intention of hope in God ﷻ and not due to a religious designation. If it is mentioned in a narration or a supplication, it is permissible to read it under the title of 'being stated in a religious designation'. And God is All-Knowing.

Eighth Question

Shaykh Muḥammad b. Muḥammad b. Nuʿmān Mufīd said in the first essay of his book, al-Mawsum: "I say that the Imāms of the household of the Prophet Muḥammad knew what went on the minds of the people. They also knew what would happen before it happened. And this is not a necessary quality nor a condition for their Imāmate; instead, God has honored them and taught them this knowledge to make their obedience and holding on to their Imāmate easier. This is not a rational necessity; it was granted and mandated to them as permission.

As for mentioning their absolute knowledge of the Unseen, it is refuted since this attribute is only given to the One who knows things by Himself and not through acquired knowledge – and this can only be said about God. The opinion above is agreed upon by a group of the followers of the Imāmate school except for those who have deviated from this school, such as those who believe in Delegation and their followers of the Exaggerators."

Doesn't this statement mentioned by the Shaykh imply the impermissibility of the absolute claim that the Imāms عليهم السلام know the Unseen?

Answer:

In the name of God ﷻ: We mentioned that they know the Unseen as much as they have been taught by God ﷻ. And the words of Shaykh Muḥammad

b. Muḥammad b. Nuʿmān Mufīd refers to absolute knowledge not limited to what we have mentioned. Moreover, it is acceptable to attribute the quality of knowledge to the person who acquires it, as attributed to the rest of the scholars. All in all, what is mentioned by Shaykh Muḥammad b. Muḥammad b. Nuʿmān Mufīd, in regards to addressing the One ﷻ who knows independently, is a form of restriction. And God is All-Knowing.

Ninth Question

It is known that Taqlīd is only permissible in matters related to the branches of faith. As for the principles of faith, such as monotheism, Prophethood, and others, they are matters which cannot undergo Taqlīd; instead, they must be studied and learned. Based on this, we understand that – as aware and well-informed youth – we have the right to express our opinions in several matters related to the principles of faith, such as monotheism, Imāmate, the virtues of the Imāms عليهم السلام, and other Islamic matters.

Moreover, from the above-mentioned principle, we can share our scholars' opinions and even disagree with them based on our analysis and knowledge; we cannot do Taqlīd in such matters.

Answer:

In the name of God ﷻ: The impermissibility of Taqlīd does not imply that you can adopt everything your reasoning has reached. Instead, one must believe and reach certainty based on correct realizations, even if they are general, such as if one knows that the knowledgeable scholars have all agreed on a particular belief regarding a specific matter and that if this belief were not correct, then they would not agree upon it. Then, this would form a general proof of the validity and righteousness of adopting that belief. And God is All-Knowing.

Tenth Question

Does the Imam's عليه السلام companions, such as Rashīd al-Ḥijrī, know of deaths and calamities?

Answer:

In the name of God ﷻ: It is well-known that some Imāms عليهم السلام taught some of their companions the knowledge of deaths and calamities, which falls under the knowledge of the Unseen that is related to death and calamities such as telling of the Imāms' ﷺ companions about the death of Mu'āwīya b. Abī Sufyān. And God is All-Knowing.

Eleventh Question

What is your opinion in regards to the narration mentioned in al-Kāfī, chapter of al-Ḥujja, a segment on the birth of Abi al-Ḥasan Mūsā b. Ja'far al-Kāẓim ﷺ, which talks about the incident where Imām Mūsā al-Kāẓim ﷺ brought a dead cow back to life. How is this balanced with the Islamic theological belief that God ﷻ is the One ﷻ who gives and takes life?

Answer:

In the name of God ﷻ: His ﷺ act of bringing something back to life takes place with God's permission ﷻ – supposing that the narration is authentic such as Prophet 'Īsā's ﷺ act of bringing dead people back to life. And God is All-Knowing.

Twelfth Question

Some narrations indicate that the Angel of Death asks for the permission of the Prophet's ﷺ and Amīr al-Mu'minīn ؑ before taking away their souls; is this true? How is this balanced with our theological belief that the angels do not disobey God ﷻ in any command and that they act upon that which they are ordered:

﴿يَخافونَ رَبَّهُم مِن فَوقِهِم وَيَفعَلونَ ما يُؤمَرونَ ۩﴾

﴿*yakhāfūna rabbahum min fawqihim wa-yaf'alūna mā yu'marūna*[a]﴾

﴿*They fear their Lord above them, and do what they are commanded*﴾[48]

Answer:

In the name of God ﷻ: There is not any contradiction in that; for if they were ordered to capture one's soul after asking for his permission,

[48] Sūrat al-Naḥl, Verse 50.

Upon recitation of this verse, one must perform sujūd/ prostration towards God ﷻ.

then they would not be disobeying God ﷻ in that command, and they would not be capturing the soul without permission. And God is All-Knowing.

Thirteenth Question

Are the names of God ﷻ exclusive, or can one call Him ﷻ by other names while taking into consideration all the aspects and conditions – for example, it must not imply his poverty or need for anything, or his immoderations or other qualities that are not appropriate to Him ﷻ?

Answer:

In the name of God ﷻ: Limiting oneself to the names mentioned in the Noble Qur'ān, the narrations, and supplication is precautionary. And God is All-Knowing.

Fourteenth Question

What is your opinion in regards to those who believe in the distortion of the Noble Qur'ān and base this belief on several narrations in Biḥār al-Anwār, al-Kāfī, and other books?

Answer:

In the name of God ﷻ.

Distortion has several meanings; some are attributed to a subject that deviated from its original truth, and some are attributed to distortion by addition or subtraction. The second part is null and void, as we mentioned in the study of the narration that tackled distortion, which is either related to the meaning as mentioned above or has a weak chain of narrations and therefore is deemed unreliable. The space given in this Q&A needs to fit further detailed clarification. And God is All-Knowing.

Fifteenth Question

It is narrated that Amīr al-Mu'minīn ﷺ said – the contextual meaning of – the following: "We are the creations of God, and the creatures are created for us."

What is the meaning of this noble ḥadīth? Some accuse the one who transferred this ḥadīth with exaggeration and disbelief – God forbid.

Answer:

In the Name of God ﷻ: This narration has not been verified through an authentic chain; however, its exoteric meaning is correct. We obey God's orders ﷻ since the creation obeys his creator. And people must obey us, whereby the Imāms عليهم السلام are guardians over the people regarding the orders and prohibitions they issue. For, God ﷻ says:

﴿أَطِيعُوا اللَّهَ وَأَطِيعُوا الرَّسُولَ وَأُولِي الأَمرِ مِنكُم﴾

﴿aṭīʿū llāha wa-ʾaṭīʿū r-rasūla wa-ʾulī l-ʾamri minkum﴾

﴿Obey God and obey the Apostle and those vested with authority among you﴾*[49]

They are the Imāms عليهم السلام – according to the Shīʿī School of Though – who were protected by God ﷻ from evil. And the Imāms عليهم السلام has two positions: the first is the position from which they clarify the Sharīʿa rulings, and the second is through which they issue orders and prohibitions – being

[49] Sūrat al-Nisāʾ, Verse 59.

* Cf. verse 4:54.

guardians – to the people. Thus, one must obey them in the latter position; and their words must be adopted in the former in pursuit of abiding by the Sharīʿa rulings and obligations. And God is All-Knowing.

Sixteenth Question

What is the Shīʿī theological belief regarding failing or frustrating deeds?

Answer:

In the name of God ﷻ: The Shīʿī theological belief aims at establishing balance. Thus, attempts to fail or frustrating actions are related to disbelief and polytheism. And God is All-Knowing.

Seventeenth Question

We read in the book "*Forty Ḥadīths*" (p. 500) by Āyatullāh Sayyid Rūhullāh Mūsawī Khumaynī the following: "In light of the fixed principles which we have verified by proof and evidence, we believe that the permissible and prohibited are both of the sustenance that is divided by God ﷻ. Moreover, we see that sins are also decreed by God ﷻ without implying the necessity of compulsion and corruption."

How can we, then, explain that the prohibited sustenance is decreed by God ﷻ? And what does it mean to say that sins are amongst God's Decree and Destiny?

Answer:

In the name of God ﷻ: God's Decree ﷻ takes place after the servant decides to accept prohibited gain. And His ﷻ destiny occurs after the servant's decree and behavior.

His ﷻ Decree and Destiny are preceded by His ﷻ knowledge of what the servant has done upon his choice and willfulness. Therefore, there is no contradiction between God's ﷻ Decree and the servant's choice, just like there is no contradiction between the servant's choice and God's ﷻ Decree. They both match each other. And God is All-Knowing.

Eighteenth Question

What is our theological belief regarding the Return (Rajʿa)? And is it one of the necessities of the Shīʿī School of Thought?

Answer:

In the name of God ﷻ: The Return is a right and is not among the necessities. It is, instead, one of the axioms according to the general opinion of scholars. And a person who does not know that it is one of the axioms does not stop – with his ignorance – outside faith and Islam. And God is the All-Knowing.

www.ingramcontent.com/pod-product-compliance
Lightning Source LLC
Chambersburg PA
CBHW031416120626
46545CB00006B/2152
9781956276404